3000 STRANGERS

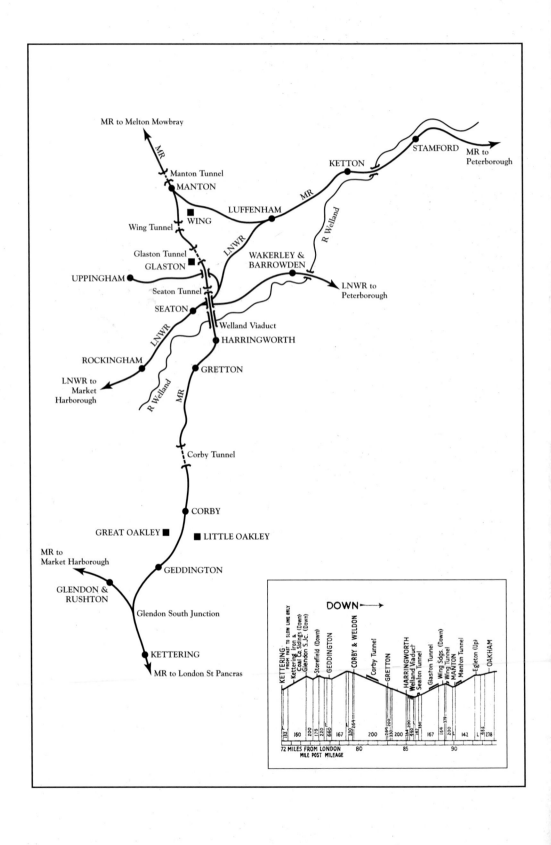

3000 STRANGERS

Navvy life on the
Kettering to Manton railway

J. Ann Paul

·RAILWAY HERITAGE·
from
The NOSTALGIA Collection

This book is dedicated to the memory of the late Rev D. W. Barrett, whose book *Life and Work Among the Navvies* launched me on my fascinating journey of discovery.

First published in 2003

British Library Cataloguing in Publication Data

A catalogue record for this book is available from the British Library.

ISBN 1 85794 212 4

Silver Link Publishing Ltd
The Trundle
Ringstead Road
Great Addington
Kettering
Northants NN14 4BW

Tel/Fax: 01536 330588
email: sales@nostalgiacollection.com
Website: www.nostalgiacollection.com

Printed and bound in Great Britain

A Silver Link book
from
The NOSTALGIA *Collection*

ACKNOWLEDGEMENTS

There are many people I would like to thank, especially those who came forward at the eleventh hour, not only with old photographs, practical help and information, but far more importantly with so much encouragement: they will know who they are. Thanks are due to the then editors of the *Stamford Mercury* and the *Grantham Journal* of the early 1990s, when I spent many happy hours among their archives. I am grateful to the staff of the Record Office for Leicestershire, Leicester and Rutland, the Northamptonshire Record Office, the Central Library Northampton, Oakham Library, and Market Harborough Library; also to Leicester City Council Museum, Market Harborough Museum and Rutland County Museum. I especially thank the staff of Peterborough Museum and Art Gallery who went to a great deal of trouble to obtain the copy of the photograph of William Connor Magee for me, and permitted it to be reproduced; the museum holds the copyright. The photograph of Rev D. W. Barrett is reproduced by permission of Rev C. Goble. For some of the old photographs I thank members of Gretton Local History Society and Rutland Local History and Record Society. For advice and information about Bishop Magee and Mrs Garnett I thank staff at Peterborough Cathedral and Ripon Cathedral. For assistance and company on my various photographic expeditions along the line over the years I thank Mr Richard Chapman, Mr David Close, and Mr Gordon Wilkinson. I extend special thanks to Captain R. E. G. Boyle for permitting access to personal family albums, and for permission to use the photographs of his ancestors, the Hon William and Lady Victoria Evans-Freke. For the photographs of Glaston Church and the Juett headstone I thank Mr Ted Reynolds. For permission to use the sketch by his late father Mr C. W. Smith, I thank Mr Michael Smith. Lastly, I thank the late Mr Jim Cliffe, who lent my family Barrett's book all those years ago, and Mr Steph Mastoris, one time curator of Market Harborough Museum, who said, 'You do realise you are writing a book don't you?' and set me on my way...

CONTENTS

'From Rushton end to Manton town, from Wing to Harper's Brook,
To nightly toil both men and boys right eagerly betook;
And bright in north, and bright in south, the glaring beacons stood,
High on the Gretton bank they shone, they shone from Corby Wood;
Far on the hills the trav'ller saw across the Rutland shire
Peak beyond peak, in dazzling blaze, the flashing sheets of fire;
The rustics left their flocks to roam by Seaton's grassy rills,
And now as miners throng'd to pierce red Glaston's claybound hills,
From Morcott's street and Preston's lanes the nightly toilers sped;
From Oakham town and Bisbrook slopes a motley throng was led.'

From *Life and Work Among the Navvies*
by Rev D. W. Barrett

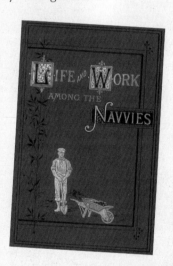

INTRODUCTION

Many years ago I read a book that I have never forgotten. It was a very battered copy of *Life and Work Among the Navvies* by Rev D. W. Barrett. It is an account not only of three vital years in the early ministry of a young Victorian curate, but also of the building of the Kettering to Manton railway. The mighty viaduct that spans the Welland Valley was frequently a focal point of family outings in my childhood. Though always drawn to my attention as 'a wonderful thing', I do not ever recall wondering why it was there, or what came before or followed after – least of all who worked to build the railway of which it was a part.

In 1990 I came upon the book again, and read it with the benefit of a lifetime of interest in local history behind me. Knowing that I had access to it for only a limited time, I took notes, for I realised that this was a unique eyewitness record about the construction, manpower and social conditions that prevailed between 1875 and 1880 in a specific situation, and in a locality that I knew intimately. Here is gentle scenery, green and spacious; a landscape of rolling hills, of wide valleys, of stone-built villages. It is a landscape enhanced rather than dominated by what I now realise is one of the wonders of the Victorian age. When viewed from many miles away the viaduct takes on a somewhat ethereal quality, especially when rising through the mists of an autumn morning. Familiar yet awe-inspiring, its huge bulk

broods over the countryside in which it stands, all three-quarters of a mile and 82 arches of it.

When I came across the book again, I became interested in the army of men, nameless and forgotten now, and those who regarded these men not just as earth-moving machines of flesh and blood, but as human beings worthy of care and consideration. Then I attempted to find out more. I began to search the shelves of the local library for anything about railway construction in general, and the building of the Kettering to Manton railway in particular, and whatever might turn up about railway navvies. I quickly discovered that little had been written about 'my line', and even less about the workforce.

Soon I found myself embarking upon an absorbing journey; a journey that had started quite by chance. There was no predetermined strategy, no setting out with a specific goal. Not having come down the academic route, I followed the interest wherever it led, whenever I had time to pursue it. I scanned indexes and footnotes, consulted bibliographies, and put in requests to the library. The requests often took months to come through. While waiting, I began to visit neighbouring libraries, and worked my way through the local history sections, seeking slim volumes on individual villages that lay along the route. I looked for notes, anecdotes – anything that might refer to the line, the navvies, and the Mission that had brought Barrett to the scene in the first place. Eventually it became clear that I was going round in a circle, for the modern authors had largely drawn from the same Victorian writers

that I had discovered for myself. Since so little
was available through the usual channels, I
abandoned the 20th century, and turned to
the local newspapers of the day, to parish
registers, and the County Record Office.
Steadily my file grew, and equally steadily my
interest increased. Then circumstances in my
own life prevented me from proceeding for
over a year, and the project was shelved.

Casually looking through what I had
acquired one day, I found that the year away
enabled me to view it objectively. I was
surprised how much information had been
accumulated. Now I could see what areas
needed strength, where there were omissions,
and what aspects required further exploration.
At last I had an aim: to write a book about the
nameless army of people who descended upon
the district, built the railway, then
disappeared. I began a process of sorting,
editing, and separating into chapters; typed up
the results and set myself a plan of action. In
earnest, when other commitments allowed, I
pursued a definite campaign. My search was
for evidence of interaction between the
railway people and the local communities; for
attitudes towards the building of the line and
the workforce. I looked for accounts of
accidents, illness, crime, the weather, the
Mission, milestones in the railway's
construction, and whatever else emerged.
Before long the navvies were no longer an
anonymous horde – some had names, as had
their wives and children. They were real
individual people, who worked, lived and in
some cases died as the railway was driven
across the green fields of Rutland and
Northamptonshire.

By this time the A6 Market Harborough
bypass, long promised, long delayed, was at
last under construction. A depot of orderly
green wooden huts was erected close to a road
junction at the outskirts of the town. Works
vehicles caused great disruption in the
neighbourhood. Enormous lorries, dozens of
them, carried equipment, spoil, rubble and
hardcore along roads and through villages
never intended for such traffic, to the
consternation of and the detriment to the
quality of life of those who lived there. Earth-
moving equipment worked like yellow ants

along the route, as for about 7 miles a narrow
scar was imposed upon the face of the
landscape. It occurred to me that there was a
parallel here, between the building of the
railways over a century ago, and the
construction of the new road networks of the
1990s. Like the Kettering and Manton
railway, the Market Harborough bypass and
the route it was to take had been the subject of
much controversy. Conflicting interests had
postponed the start of both projects for many
years. Vested interests were aired, alternative
routes considered, plans rejected and
reviewed. Once begun, there was a great
striving to get the job done. Yet there is one
particular difference. There were
comparatively few men employed to build the
bypass, and the majority of them drove home
when the day's work was done. But when the
railway was built all those years before,
manpower, not machines, was the force
behind the great Victorian enterprise. This is
why more than 3,000 men came to toil across
the valleys and through the hills.

Nearly a century and a quarter have passed.
The men themselves are largely forgotten.
Though the evidence of their labour remains,
the remarkable achievement is taken for
granted – I took it for granted myself. This line
is still in use, though it has mellowed, and
become part of the landscape, while so many
others have ceased to be. We see so much of
the rail network that brought prosperity in the
past now disused and abandoned. Many
hundreds of miles have sunk, as it were, back
into the landscape in which they were built.
They have become havens for wildlife:
flowers, butterflies, birds and badgers. Yet the
building of the railways transformed the
economy and the quality of life to an extent
never before seen in history. For the first time
communication was no longer dependent
upon the power of the horse, and the rhythm
of the planet – the wind and the tide. We see
the old scenes of industry fallen to ruin; the
canals either decayed and overgrown or given
over to pleasure and recreation. When we
consider the outstanding feats of engineering
skill and enterprise achieved during the last
200 years – in industry, in transportation, in
communication – famous names spring to

Above The magnificent viaduct completely dominates the countryside in which it stands, yet its effect is strangely beautiful in the wide valley. *Author's collection*

Below The 3.15pm from St Pancras crosses the Welland Viaduct into Rutland on its way to Bradford behind 'Jubilee' Class 4-6-0 No 45627 *Sierra Leone*. *Arthur and Elisabeth Jordan collection*

mind: Arkwright, Brunel, Macadam. There are many more. We are aware of the inventors, the planners, the innovators, the men of vision, those who recognised not only the possibilities but also the demands that new industries would make. How often do we reflect upon the men whose labour and lives brought these visions to reality?

A vast roving multitude travelled the kingdom and beyond to build with their own physical strength and skill the foundations upon which the present day is based. They dug and burrowed, moved earth and rock, built embankments, drove cuttings, mined tunnels … and not only for the canals and railways. They worked on the expanding road systems, the reservoirs, the waterworks, the docks, the piers – all to support the burgeoning industries and the growing towns. They cleared immense spaces for the Victorians to build their cities upon, and sank the sewers and subways that ran beneath. The wealth of the nation depended on them, yet they were for the most part feared and despised. Little is written about them as people, and a hundred or so years later they are as anonymous as the Israelites who built the pyramids. Men of many trades and skills, they are instantly recognised by the one word: Navvies.

I turn again to Barrett's book. First published in 1879, the third edition in 1883, its declared intention was to 'supply a record of a special undertaking in railway work, and an account of the manner and customs of the navvies…' The declared intention of my book is to draw attention once again to these people, and to recall in some measure aspects of the men and their families who came to work and live in the district, whose presence in such huge numbers made so great an impact on the rural communities, and the result of whose labour brought prosperity to the region for generations to come.

I will be looking in detail at the building of one line in particular, a line that had been considered too difficult and expensive to construct at all. The years in question are from 1874, when the Act of Parliament was obtained, to 1880, when the line was fully operational. There will, however, be brief sorties into earlier years, while the scene is being set. For the most part the information used has been trawled from the archives of the *Grantham Journal* and the then *Lincoln, Rutland and Stamford Mercury* of 1874-80, parish records, and three Victorian authors: Rev D. W. Barrett, F. S. Williams, and Mrs Elizabeth Garnett.

This railway will speak for the courage and prodigious feats of strength and endurance showed by a class of men largely feared by the general public of their day, and the results of whose labour is largely taken for granted in ours. In fewer than 16 miles most of the hazards and obstacles, achievements and failures, likely to be met with while building a railway in the late 19th century were encountered.

The more I find out about the railway navvies of the Kettering to Manton line, the more I feel their story must be told. And by the end of this book, many will have emerged from the past as people, with names. Many more, the majority, will not – though their work is there to remember them by. The line completed, most of them moved on. Some gave up their wandering life and raised their families here. Some claimed six feet of the red earth of Rutland or Northamptonshire clay for ever.

1
PROLOGUE: WAS THERE LIFE BEFORE THE RAILWAYS?

Times change. Our cities, towns and villages suffer so much from the congestion of traffic in the early years of the 21st century, and bypass after bypass continue to be constructed to channel the bulk of it around the built-up areas. Efforts are constantly made to improve the flow, to divert, to reduce speed. These efforts frequently generate protests. There are those who courageously take on the urgent and sometimes violent defence of an irreplaceable natural feature or historic site. Others may be more passive, yet still of the 'not in my back yard' opinion.

In the villages schools have closed, as have shops, post offices, and other amenities. Whole communities, once adequately provided for within their own locality, their necessary journeys amply accommodated by the railway and bus services, now find themselves, as it were, marooned. Yet people must shop, bank, visit the doctor and so on. Few of those employed now work close to where they live. Husbands and wives often travel in different directions. More than one car per household is often indispensable. Once a cross between a luxury and a workhorse, the family car is now for many people the only vital link between home and everything else. Children in many rural districts have to travel many miles to school. My own children faced a daily journey of over an hour, as the school bus wound its circuitous way between the villages.

Mighty 'juggernauts' manoeuvre themselves along roads that were never intended for such vehicles. Agricultural machinery is wider, longer, heavier than ever before, and must use the roads. And so we live in the era of the family car, and of freight of every description hauled by road from one end of the nation to the other. Ease and safety of personal travel is not only an accepted aspect of life in the present day, but two generations have grown up with the greater proportion of the communications network served by the road transport system with virtually no alternative. Though we may deplore the effect of the ever-increasing traffic and all it involves, we still expect to set out on our routine journeys, and arrive safely at our destinations.

Travellers of old

The ancient trackways of pre-history, the forest paths, saltways and drift roads gave way to the fine roads made by the Romans, roads constructed with such skill that many routes of the present day are laid on their foundations, or follow their courses. There were great difficulties and dangers to be overcome, but it was not such a static population as may be supposed. People travelled about in great numbers, even in medieval times. The court was constantly in progress, armies were on the march, and bishops and their retinues made visitations around their diocese. Pilgrims made long treks to the holy sites both in this country and abroad. Judges with their clerks went to the various seats of law. Peddlers peddled, and wandering workers followed employment. People went to market their wares, to purchase provisions, to visit.

However, by the end of the 17th century

the roads had deteriorated to little more than open spaces over which there was the right to travel. Relays of pack-horses were the main means of transporting coal, merchandise and other goods, while on the whole other journeys were undertaken on horseback or on foot, at great danger, it must be said, to the travellers. There were wheeled vehicles, but the state of the roads made for very troublesome journeys. Ladies frequently rode side-saddle, but more commonly upon pillions seated behind a friend or a servant. There is a reference to this in *Our Iron Roads* by Frederick S. Williams (1852), where the author describes it as being '...very agreeable for a lady to be married in her riding habit, and jog off for her honeymoon on her pillion, with her arm around her husband's waist'.

It may have been very agreeable, but a description of the roads at the end of the 18th century indicates that it was probably preferable to travelling by coach: 'Some of them had ruts four feet deep by measure, and into these ruts huge stones were dropped to enable wagons to pass at all; and these in their turn broke their axles by the horrible jolting, so that within eighteen miles I saw three wagons lying in this condition.' (Arthur Young, *Tours*)

And these were the highways. The common roads were worse, for little effort was made to mend them at this time. Likewise, the streets in the towns were similarly neglected. At Oakham, for example, the county town of Rutland, the inhabitants were summoned to Quarter Sessions in 1775, for a certain road in that town was '...in such decay for want of due reparation and amendment that the liege subjects of our Lord the King through the same way with their horses, coaches, carts, and carriages could not go, return, pass, ride and labour without great danger to their lives and loss of their Goods.' Travellers were often forced to dismount, and 'quagmires, sloughs and bogs enveloped horses to the withers'. There was much loss of life through coaches overturning. The lot of the traveller was not a happy one.

In reply to certain yearnings expressed by some of his contemporaries for a time that had passed for ever, F. S. Williams, writing in the 1870s, described a more authentic representation of what he called the coaching days of old:

'Stories are told of dreary waitings at road-sides in the small hours of wintry mornings for coaches which, when they arrived, were full; of how travellers could not keep awake and dared not go to sleep; of roads infamously bad, which the whole range of language could not sufficiently describe; and of additional and exciting perils ever and anon of a race betwixt two stagecoaches, in which the lives of thirty or forty distressed or helpless individuals were at the mercy of two intoxicated brutes. To be perched for perhaps twenty hours, exposed to all weathers, on the outside of a coach, trying in vain to find a soft seat, sitting now with the face and now with the back to the wind, rain, or sun; to endure long and wretched winter nights, when the passenger was half starved with cold and the other half with hunger, was a miserable undertaking, and was often looked forward to with no small anxiety by many whose business required them frequently to travel. Nor were the inside passengers much more agreeably accommodated. To be closely packed in a little straight-backed vehicle, where the limbs could not be in the least extended, nor the wearied frame indulged by any change of posture, was felt by many to be a distressing experience, while the constantly recurring demands of driver and guard, and the exactions of innkeepers, often destroyed the last traces of the fancied romance of stage-coach travelling. Truth to say, modern wayfarers have little conception of what travelling used to be. It killed hundreds of people; and often in winter a man would get so nearly frozen to death that he could only be got down from the top of a coach in the bent position into which he had stiffened. The railroad grumblers of today know nothing of the sufferings of their Spartan forefathers'. (F. S. Williams, *Our Iron Roads*)

Clearly the Christmas card image we fondly retain of a stagecoach bowling along, horses at full gallop, the smiling rosy-cheeked passengers glowing with excitement, the post-horn sounding a gay warning to the jolly innkeeper of an imminent arrival, was far from reality.

A survey of agriculture, made in 1808, records that the roads of Rutland were so bad that travellers were obliged to keep the wheels in the ruts, when '... a chaise and pair ... go jostling one against the other, and keep slipping into the deep ruts, and are thus liable to fall every step they take.' (Richard Parkinson)

Every parish was required and bound to repair highways within its boundaries, and parishioners were obliged to give gratuitous labour six days a year. Nevertheless the strains imposed on the small communities were considerable. A sparsely populated district through which a major road passed could not keep it in good order by this means; the parishes had not sufficient resources, either in labour or finance. This was the case with Rutland, where a stretch of the Great North Road carried heavy traffic between York and London.

The coming of the railway age

However, the coming of the railways and the development of the system not only brought the reality of inexpensive and swift movement of goods and passengers, but also contributed greatly to the prosperity of the nation. Amidst the cheers of many and the trepidations of not a few, on 27 September 1825 a single locomotive, driven by no less a person than George Stephenson himself, moved away from Stockton on its newly built track. The 'Railway Age' proper had begun. The train comprised six wagons of coal and flour, then a covered coach in which travelled directors and other worthies, followed by 21 coal wagons (minus coal), suitably modified to accommodate the many passengers that filled them. Finally, there were six more wagons laden with coal. In all, the 450 passengers and freight totalled 90 tons, all safely transported by locomotive No 1.

F. S. Williams wrote:

'Off started the procession, with a horseman carrying a flag at its head. A great concourse of people stood along the line. Many of them tried to accompany it by running, and some gentlemen on horseback galloped across the fields to keep up with the engine. The railway descending with a gentle incline towards Darlington, the rate of speed was consequently variable. At a favourable part of the road, Stephenson determined to try the speed of the engine, and he called upon the horseman to get out of the way. And Stephenson put on the speed to twelve miles, and then to fifteen miles an hour, and the runners on foot, and the gentlemen on horseback, and the horseman with the flag, were soon far behind.' (*Our Iron Roads*)

Changing attitudes

There had been much doubt and ridicule as to the viability of the enterprise; fear that a lack of demand for horses would bring ruin, that the mortgagees of the tolls on the turnpikes would suffer, that stagecoaches would be bereft of business. Indeed, the Stockton & Darlington proposal was presented to Parliament three times before the Bill was passed and the Act obtained. In 1874 the Kettering to Manton scheme was to suffer similar delays, as vested interests were aired and difficulties presented, although by the time this railway was under serious consideration there had been a considerable change in public feeling towards the railways, as we will see in Chapter 2. Until the benefits that outweighed the prejudices became obvious, for many the coming of the railways was far from welcome. To use the parlance of our modern era, the attitude of many people of influence had indeed been 'not in my back yard'. The alarm of those with personal and financial interests for the continuance of existing systems elsewhere, and the lengths to which they would go to prevent what we now regard as progress, makes amusing reading. Nevertheless, it was then of serious concern.

To recall some of the objections:

'A rumour that it was proposed to bring such a thing as a railroad within a dozen miles of a particular neighbourhood, was sufficient to elicit adverse petitions to Parliament, and public subscriptions were opened to give effect to the opposition... Householders were told that their homes were hourly in danger of being burned to the ground, and farmers were assured that their hens would not lay or their cows graze, and that game would fall dead to the ground if they attempted to fly over the poisoned breath exhaled by the engines... Hundreds of innkeepers and thousands of horses would have nothing to do ... canals would be destroyed and those who lived by them would become beggars ... the 27,000 miles of turn-pike roads in Great Britain would be made useless ... medical men asserted that the gloom and damp of tunnels, the deafening peal, the clanking chains, and the dismal glare of the locomotives would be disastrous alike to body and mind...'

Northampton was opposed to the London & Birmingham line (the wool of the sheep would be injured by the smoke of the locomotives). The progress of the Great Western was impeded by Oxford and Eton (anybody acquainted with the nature of Eton boys would know that they could not be kept from the railway if it was allowed to be constructed). But, as Williams pointed out, in the preamble of the first Act it was stated that the line would be 'of great public utility, by facilitating the conveyance of coal, iron, lime, corn, and other commodities'.

Although the railways were primarily considered as the means by which raw materials and finished goods would be swiftly and economically transported, passengers soon insisted on being carried regularly. But, Williams continued, prejudice, vested interests and abuse could not avert the advance of the railways. Farmers could buy their coals, lime and manure with less money, and could find readier access to the best markets for their produce. Cows still gave milk, sheep fed and fattened, and at length even skittish horses ceased to shy at the passing trains. It is almost impossible now to appreciate the impact for the better the coming of the railways had.

Thirty years later, the promoters of the Kettering to Manton railway succeeded in persuading those with vested interests what great benefit the new railway would bring to the neighbourhood. The shareholders were rallied, the capital raised, the Royal Assent obtained, and the route defined. The work was to proceed. But the consequence of this was that the quiet country parishes would be inundated by some 4,000 railway people – men, women and children. This invasion was preceded by such a reputation of lawlessness as to instil dread into all but the most stalwart heart, whether or not that reputation was justified. Many of the prejudices, objections, and in some circumstances very real fears towards the navvies – the legacy of the canal age and the early days of railway building – still existed. Furthermore, the local resources would be stretched to the limits, as we shall see.

2
WAS ANOTHER RAILWAY REALLY NECESSARY?

Obviously the navvies had come for a reason: to build the railway. And the railway was to be built for pressing reasons too. The proposal was not conjured out of the air. It is important therefore to place the Kettering to Manton line in the scheme of things, so for the moment we leave the navvies and look into why such a new and expensive plan was justified.

Many projects had been under serious consideration to provide railway communication for this part of the Midlands, some dating from as far back as the 1840s. They fell either because of lack of local financial support or because alternative north-south routes, though desirable, were deemed to be impracticable. For example, a proposition was put forward by the Northampton, Lincoln & Hull Railway Company in 1845 for a line to run from Northampton, on through Kettering, Uppingham, Oakham and Grantham to Lincoln, where a branch line would connect these places with the growing port of Grimsby. Another plan proposed a line from Lincoln to join the Midland line near Market Harborough, and so on southwards. The name of this scheme, originally called the Hull, Great Grimsby & Southampton Direct Railway, was later changed to the Lincoln & Northampton Railway. The possibility was investigated that it should go via Grantham, Oakham, Uppingham and Rockingham, but this too was not developed further. However, by the early 1870s once again there was considerable interest in the region.

Why was another length of railway considered necessary, when a spider's web of iron already connected one part of the nation with another? In the opening paragraph of *Life and Work Among the Navvies*, Rev D. W. Barrett provides an explanation :

'A glance at an ordinary railway map will soon show the object the promoters of the Kettering and Manton Railway had in view, when they determined to add one more avenue to the closely tangled mesh of iron roads which already intersect our country. A more direct and expeditious route from the North to London was desired; and several companies had, in years gone by, surveyed the district lying between Nottingham and Kettering, with the view of forming a connecting line with their respective systems; but it was not until 1874, and then only after difficulty and opposition, that a Bill was obtained by the enterprising Directors of the Midland Company, and the line finally decided on. What were several thousands of pounds, or even a few millions, in order to shorten the distance when other lines were competing in the race to London? The route from Carlisle could be lessened by about thirty-five miles, and the work must be done.'

There certainly was considerable opposition. The Bill was before Parliament for 40 days. Then it went up to the House of Lords, where it was mutilated further. Eventually it had the Royal Assent, and the Midland obtained the Act. Barrett's explanation was, no doubt, sufficient for his contemporaries. They would be aware of the many issues that had been addressed. But since then a century and a half has elapsed, and perhaps further explanation is now necessary.

The rival schemes and railway politics of the 1840s, which became popularly known as the 'Railway Mania', have been dealt with at great length by many historians, and it is not intended to reiterate these in this book, other than to record that by the 1870s, when it was realised that the proposed Kettering to Manton line may become viable, the smaller companies had for the most part either merged or closed down entirely, and the several local companies jostling to control the Midlands had been absorbed by the four principal protagonists. Of these, the Great Northern and Midland companies fought a bitter duel to obtain the business of the great industrialists, and to woo the custom of the travelling public. This was particularly the case between 1872 and 1875. The press recorded every thrust and parry between these two mighty organisations, as they strove to secure the business nationwide. We will look into this more closely later in the chapter.

In the early 1870s, many threads, economic and social, had interwoven to create the need for additional north-south railway communication through the region. The transportation of minerals was the prime concern. The industrial cities of northern England and the Midlands were expanding rapidly, as was the associated demand for coal, iron and other minerals. The main line between Derby and Leicester, controlled by the Great Northern and over which the Midland had running powers, was frequently affected by expensive though inevitable delays.

Whether or not we believe in the Industrial Revolution, and many historians challenge the concept, the fact remains that as the demands of the rapidly developing industrial centres increased, so the need for minerals was stimulated. Industry, iron, coal and railways – they were all inextricably linked. The railway companies vied with each other in building more lines to accommodate the burgeoning business. The Midland and Great Northern, in direct competition, both

sought additional routes in the region. Their surveyors and civil engineers, engaged in geological investigations further and deeper into virgin railway territory, found valuable deposits of minerals at the very time the requirements of industry seemed to be insatiable. As cuttings were dug and tunnels were driven through the countryside of middle England, even more rich sources were discovered. Thus the vast extent of the mineral wealth that lay beneath the rolling acres became apparent, though its extent was not yet realised.

A 'chicken and egg' situation was created. The iron-masters needed coal to produce the iron. More access to the coal and iron-ore fields was called for, and the building of additional railways was necessary. Iron was needed to build the new 'iron roads', and coal to produce the steam, not only to drive the locomotives, but also as the basis for power in industry.

An article from *The Builder* was printed in the *Stamford Mercury* on 1 March 1872 and illustrates these points most graphically:

'It has lately been shown that 14,247 miles of railway are now being worked on in the United Kingdom, on which have been expended no less than £500,000,000, which is five times the amount of the annual value of the real property of Great Britain, and two thirds of the National Debt. The gross net annual revenue of the railways in this country, after deducting all working expenses, exceeds £20,000,000 sterling, more than the told revenue, from all sources, of Belgium, Holland, Portugal, Denmark, Sweden, and Norway. The companies have in their direct employment more than 100,000 officers and servants. The value of the rolling stock exceeds £30,000,000. The consumption of coal and coke by railway engines amounts to between 2,000,000 and 3,000,000 tons a year: so that in every minute of time throughout the year about four tons of coal are consumed, and twenty tons of water are flashed into steam. The consumption of fuel is about equal to the amount of coal exported from Great Britain to foreign countries. There are more than 3,000,000 tons of iron laid down in rail alone, and the chairs would weigh nearly 1,000,000 tons: so that there are not far short of 4,000,000 tons of iron on the permanent ways of the United Kingdom, and of these about 30,000 tons of rail have to be each year replaced.'

On 29 May 1874 the *Stamford Mercury* made the following announcement: 'Two seams of coal 2ft and 7ft respectively have been discovered on the estate of Mr H. O. Shore, near Leicester. The seams are believed to extend through Bagworth, Newbold, Peckleton, Desford and Newton, to Ratby. It is conjectured that the whole of the Leicestershire coal will soon be found.' New collieries were opening in quick succession. Five months later came the report: 'DISCOVERY OF COAL – The welcome intelligence was brought to Newark on Wednesday that coal had been discovered at the borings of the South Scarle and Swinderby Coal Exploration Company. They are situate near to the Midland Railway, about 7 miles from Newark.' Some 127,000,000 tons of coal were transported by rail in 1874.

Meanwhile, to the south of the region, production from the iron-ore fields was developing rapidly, though the size of the ore-bearing district was not yet fully understood. It was to be found far and away more extensive than had previously been imagined, due directly to the building of the Kettering to Manton line, when rich deposits were revealed. It must be pointed out that though the line had everything to do with ironstone and iron works, the object was not to find the ore – it was discovered during the construction of the line.

A further consideration was that although more powerful locomotives were being built to accommodate the longer and heavier mineral trains, progress was impeded by the gradients of the existing lines. Time, then as now, was money, and greater demands on too few tracks made costly delays inevitable. It became imperative that new routes, expensive though

they would be, should be built to meet the needs of the age. And, as we have seen, at the very time the requirements of industry seemed to be insatiable, the surveyors and civil engineers engaged in the exploration of possible new routes in the region discovered during their geological investigations how rich and extensive were the deposits of minerals.

Opening up the region

The district that lies near the heart of England had long been an area under consideration by the leading railway companies. It was desirable not only to improve communications between the North and London, but also to connect the ports of the East Coast with the industrial Midlands. The London & North Western Railway wanted a better route to Nottingham and the coalfields. Nottingham, by now becoming one of the foremost industrial cities, and placed as it was close to the coal, was at that time only served by a branch line. The Great Northern Railway, in direct competition with the Midland, was concerned with the 'race to London', the mineral business, and improved access to Leicester, also fast becoming one of the major industrial centres. The Midland's prime interest was in the exploitation of the iron-ore deposits of Leicestershire, Northamptonshire and Rutland, and also the vast coalfields to the north of the region. Indeed, all the major companies planned to exploit the rich mineral resources. The Manchester, Sheffield & Lincolnshire Railway also sought any means of reaching the South and the Capital; in 1894 it was to begin its 'London Extension', England's last trunk line southwards towards London. While that new line was under construction, the company changed its name to Great Central.

There were yet more considerations in support of the need for additional railway communications. The growing urban population, divorced from its agricultural roots, must be fed. Produce and fuel had to be brought into the cities, but it was costly to transport such goods from stations on the existing lines. Everything had to be taken by horse and cart to and from the railway stations. Additional routes through rural districts, with stations close to the small agricultural communities, would provide faster means of transporting milk, cattle, sheep, pigs, grain and other produce right into the towns. At the same time the freight costs of coal and other essential commodities to the country districts would be much reduced because they would not have to be hauled so far. There would be benefits all round, but at a price.

Leading up to the time when the Midland obtained the royal assent for the Kettering and Manton line, there were rapid developments. Most specifically was the contention between the Great Northern and the Midland to open up the territory between Nottingham and Kettering. As we have seen, this district was crucial, because of its proximity both to the mineral fields and to the industrial centres. However, it presented many problems. It was a region that had been considered almost too difficult and prohibitively too costly through which to build a railway. A point frequently raised was that any new line that crossed from north to south would have to traverse the grain of the land, for all the valleys run from west to east. However, if the physical and financial difficulties could be overcome, the gains would be enormous. By the early 1870s, technology had advanced, demands increased, and the project was deemed feasible. Both the directors of the Midland and the Great Northern introduced similar schemes to develop the region. The proposed Kettering to Manton line, then, was not an isolated project, but was a vital component in the Midland's overall strategy.

Reasons for the route

Although the promoters of the Kettering to Manton railway had put forward their project many times in the past, it had not been accepted as a viable proposition. Speculative surveys were discouraging, for they showed that the region presented many natural difficulties that would make the desired north-south route prohibitively costly. Shareholders

were reluctant to invest the necessary capital such expansion would entail, and the various schemes were put to one side. By the early 1870s, however, commercial interests and economic pressures, some of which we have already looked into, encouraged urgent review. The Directors of the Midland Railway recognised a great opportunity. One potential route is recorded in the 'Accounts of Public Undertakings: Midland Railways', under 'Newark, Melton Mowbray, and Leicester Railways: Midland Railway Nottingham to Rushton':

'No 195. 30th November 1871. DESCRIPTION: Newark, Melton Mowbray, and Leicester Railways. Duplicate of 193.

2(a) Manton and Rushton Line – from a junction with the Syston and Peterborough line in the parish of Manton (Rutland) to a junction with the Leicester to Hitchin line in the township of Barford, (Northants), crossing Leicestershire through the parishes of Great Easton and Bringhurst. Total length 14 miles 5 furlongs 1 chain.

2(b) Manton Curve – From a junction with the Syston to Peterborough line to join the said Manton to Rushton line, all in the parish of Wing (Rutland). Total length 3 furlongs 5 chains.'

To compare the final scheme as laid before Parliament some three years later with that proposed in (2a) above is an interesting though frustrating speculation without the benefit of a plan. By what means, for example, was the line to cross Rutland from Wing into Leicestershire, to arrive at the parishes of Great Easton and Bringhurst and then on into Northamptonshire? It would certainly be west of the present course, and possibly run between Lyddington and Stoke Dry, entering Leicestershire in the area now inundated by the Eye Brook Reservoir. There it was in the parish of Great Easton and then it would have passed through to that of Bringhurst. It would have to cross the Welland to enter

Northamptonshire probably somewhere between the parishes of Cottingham and Rockingham, approximately 5 miles west of the present line. If so, it would also have to cross the estates of Rockingham Castle, on its way to join the Leicester to Hitchin line at 'the township of Barford', then as now a scattered hamlet to the east of Rushton. If this was the case, no doubt that was where the main unnamed landowner's objections lay, as we see below. If adopted, this plan would have been some 2½ miles shorter than the final scheme. However, this proposal was abandoned, as were several others, and the final route, as laid before Parliament and accepted, took quite a different course.

The additional 'more direct and expeditious route' from the North to London was now deemed essential to accommodate the expanding business, but much survey work was undertaken before the final course was decided upon. The Midland proposed that two new lines be built in connection with each other. The first, from Nottingham to Melton Mowbray, would run on to the existing Midland line from Syston (Leicester) to Peterborough, through Manton Tunnel. From the south side of the tunnel, at the same time, the other new line would strike across the countryside approximately due south for nearly 16 miles, to just north of Kettering, there to join the trunk line to London. By these means, if the Act of Parliament was attained, the Midland Railway Company would achieve a new main route, with improved gradients, over its own metals, directly from Nottingham to Kettering; a great advantage over its competitors.

Landowners' attitudes

There certainly was, as Barrett said, difficulty and opposition when the Bill went before the various parliamentary committees. The *Grantham Journal* of 6 June 1874 published without comment the following report, which indicates some of the local issues that had been addressed when one route was abandoned and another accepted. Here we have a fascinating glimpse into the workings of a Parliamentary Committee:

'THE MIDLAND RAILWAY BILL: The Committee of the House of Commons appointed to consider the conditions of the bill proceeded with their investigation on Tuesday, Mr Beach in the Chair. Mr Cripps, QC (with him Mr Bidden, QC) said that the committee was aware that this was an omnibus bill, and that many sections of it were opposed. The first one of these, which was opposed by a landowner of the district, was the project on the part of the Midland Railway Company to construct a line of rail thirteen miles in length, which was to be laid down between Manton in Rutland and Rushton, in Northamptonshire. This district was peculiarly destitute of Railway accommodation, and Lady Cardigan, who resided at Deene, was obliged to go to Kettering, a distance of twelve miles, to get a train to London. A place named Corby was greatly inconvenienced by having no direct railway communication. He would not occupy the time of the Committee but called Mr Bennett. Mr Bennett said that he was a land agent, and acted as such on the estate of Lady Cardigan. He, on her behalf, entirely approved the new line. Cross examined, Mr Bennett said that the Countess of Cardigan had to go twelve miles from Deene to Kettering, where the first station was. If they went to Rockingham they were going away from London. They intended, if the line was made, to go to the station at Seaton. They wished to have a station at Corby, but the whole of the district through which the proposed line passed would be benefited by it as well as Corby. In 1872, he was not consulted about the line in question at all, but did not oppose it. The bill then was different from this in some details. Mr Trefuis said he was a general land agent residing in Bedfordshire, and he had carefully studied the whole district through which the proposed line was to pass, and was of the opinion that it was of great importance to the district, and hoped that the Committee would

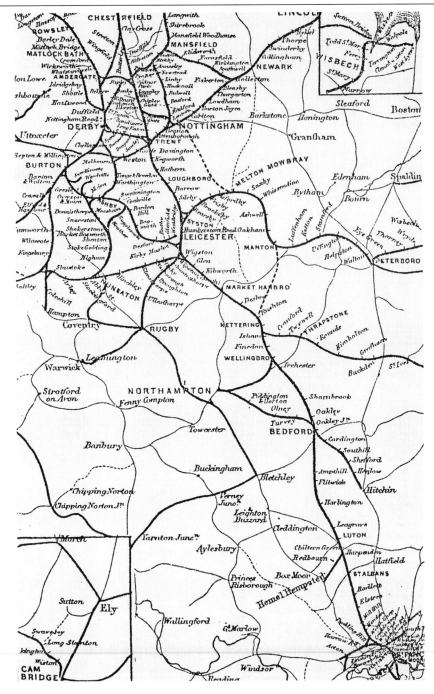

This railway map of 1871 shows the 'spider's web of iron' around the cities of the Midlands. The Midland Railway's proposed new routes between Nottingham and Melton Mowbray, and between Manton and Kettering, are marked by heavy dotted lines. The rival scheme of the Great Northern Railway, from Newark through Melton Mowbray to Market Harborough, is shown by the lighter dots. *From* The Midland Railway: Its Rise and Progress *by F. S. Williams (1876)*

approve it. After additional evidence had been given on behalf of the promoter's case, witnesses were called to support the case of the opponents of the bill. The Committee, at a late hour, after a brief consultation, found for the promoters of the bill, and the clauses were gone through and passed.'

Lady Cardigan was the widow of the 7th Earl of Cardigan, he who 20 years earlier had led the 'Gallant Six Hundred' at Balaklava. She was one of the principal landowners through whose property the proposed line would pass. I suspect that the unnamed 'landowner of the district' who had opposed the 1872 proposal was the owner of Rockingham Castle, and I think that one of the objectors of the accepted Kettering to Manton route may well have been the Earl of Lonsdale – the famous 'Yellow Earl'. He was not only one of the foremost landowners in Rutland, but also held extensive estates in Westmorland (as it was then). I base this supposition on the fact that when the line was under construction he appeared in the courts several times in direct conflict both with the railway company and the contractors.

But times were changing. And so were attitudes. The frame of mind that had led to the so-called 'Battle of Saxby' recounted by many railway historians, and which had taken place only a few miles from Manton in 1844, had become more forward-looking. By the time the promoters of the Kettering to Manton line were prepared to revive their scheme, many landowners in the Midlands were eager to become part of the rapid developments. Some indeed, who had hitherto been opposed to railways passing close by or across their estates, now saw that great profit could be made by co-operation with the railway companies. Moreover, fortunes were waiting should mineral deposits be found beneath their rolling acres. For example, the then Duke of Rutland at first resisted the coming of a railway, but when surveys revealed the rich coal and ironstone deposits on his estates, he realised the implications – the presence of mineral wealth combined with projected accessibility to the

rail network – and did a complete 'U turn'. Land ownership itself was changing at this time. Some large hereditary estates, affected by among other things the serious situation in agriculture, were actually being sold off, and were purchased by wealthy industrial magnates with vested interests both in the exploitation of the mineral fields and the advance of the railways.

Another powerful social and economic influence may perhaps not readily come to mind in modern times. This is the area of the country famous as 'The Shires', the home of some of the oldest and most prestigious hunts in the kingdom, and one of the reasons why railway development in the region was confined to a great extent to the last quarter of the century. When railways first came to the region, the powerful hunting fraternity was hostile, and brought its authority to bear in curtailing further expansion. The hunting interest did not long present an inhibiting front, however. A very strong lobby encouraged the railways because they provided convenient access from the cities to the heart of the hunting shires. Special trains were arranged in the season, and Williams wrote, 'Hunters [that is to say the horses] walk in and out of their railway boxes as quietly as though they were the holders of season tickets.' The House of Lords supported the Newark to Melton Mowbray section of the Great Northern Railway against leading competitors precisely because of the importance of the hunts. Once again, a notable opponent was the Earl of Lonsdale.

Rivals for the territory

By the 1860s it was not only considered necessary to transport the coal to the ironworks, instead of the reverse, as had formerly been the case, but also the means had to be provided for doing so. The railway companies quickly realised the potential, and vied with each other to take advantage of the urgent business. As we saw earlier, by early 1870s several companies were involved in schemes to open up the region, some of which we now consider in more detail, for they were the forerunners of the eventually successful

Kettering to Manton project. They followed one another with bewildering rapidity, and the press reported every move.

In 1872 the Midland Railway Company obtained the Royal Assent for a line to run from Nottingham to Saxby, and on the same day the Great Northern obtained one for a line between Newark and the tiny hamlet of Marefield, en route to Leicester. The intense rivalry between the Directors of the two companies, the principal protagonists in the competition for the development of the region, was reaching a climax when, in the *Grantham Journal* of 11 July 1874, an article appeared from which I have extracted relevant portions, for they support points I have made in this chapter:

'NEW RAILWAY COMMUNICATION: After three years fighting, the Great Northern Railway Company have succeeded in carrying Bills through Parliament for making a line of railway from Newark to Leicester and Market Harborough. The effect of this will be to open up the great coal-field in the Erewash Valley in Derbyshire, to the whole of the Great Northern and London North Western systems, which have been almost exclusively in the hands of the Midland Company. A direct communication is given to Melton, Leicester, and all the towns and districts lying south of these, with the Yorkshire and other markets in the north of England. We are also informed that the Great Northern Company will commence making the line as soon as the harvest is in…'

The locally promoted Newark & Leicester Railway Company was taken over by the Great Northern, and in its turn this company was joined by the London & North Western, to extend its line to Market Harborough. The Midland had previously joined the Manchester, Sheffield & Lincolnshire in promoting a line from Doncaster to Rushton, to counter the Great Northern and London & North Western's Nottingham to Market Harborough route. Although this scheme had

been authorised in 1873, it was considered impracticable, and had been abandoned. Now it was revived, and the report above caused much consternation within the ranks of the Midland shareholders. A further threat to the Midland's mineral business was made six weeks later when this article in the *Stamford, Rutland and Lincolnshire Mercury* of 21 August 1874 appeared:

'A NEW RAILWAY – The proposed railway from the Great Eastern system, running directly northwards to Oundle, east of Nottingham, through Mansfield and Swinton on the one hand, and Ollerton, Tickhill and Doncaster on the other, will shorten the route between London and the North considerably. The proposal is taken up warmly by the land, coal and mineral owners, and meetings in favour of the new line have been held in the locality. The direction of the line has been laid out, and it is estimated by Mr Hamilton Fulton, the Engineer, that the cost will not exceed £22,000 per mile. With the present amount of experience and competition amongst contractors, notwithstanding the existing high prices, it is alleged that at no former period could the engineering works be executed at less cost, provided the works as executed are properly supervised and periodically paid for in cash and not in shares. Should the traffic on the new line be only two-thirds that of the Midland Railway, upon Mr Fulton's estimated outlay it is said the return would be 7½% per annum.'

And so we see the emergence of a shorter route between London and the North becoming an important factor. The Midland was put on its mettle, and swiftly countered the move less than a month later, when the *Stamford Mercury* reported on 25 September 1874:

'THE RAILWAY NEWS advocates the purchase of the London, Chatham, and Dover Railway by the Midland Railway Company, to complete the "backbone of

England". One company, from Dover to Carlisle, with metropolitan stations at St Pancras, Holborn Viaduct, Ludgate Hill, Victoria, and a host of less important points, is declared to be a scheme worthy of the Midland, and one that can be carried out with perfect satisfaction to the Chatham shareholders, while absolutely without risk of loss and with great future profit to the Midland Company. At the same time it would be popular with everybody...'

Although neither the Midland Railway nor the Kettering to Manton line are mentioned in the following article, comparisons can be drawn. Many of the issues discussed so far are illustrated very well by this authentic 'voice from the past'. Here is outspoken frustration expressed by a leading figure as a consequence of the rejection by the Upper House of a railway scheme:

'RAILWAY ACCOMMODATION FOR HULL AND NORTH LINCOLNSHIRE: A correspondent of the Eastern County News (North Lincoln) says: "In laying the foundation stone of the Barton-on-Humber Literary Institute last week, Mr John Hope Barton of Saxby Hall, a large landed proprietor, alluded to the late scheme of a tunnel under the Humber to connect Hull and Lincolnshire with the great railway systems of the South and West of England. The possibility of such a tunnel, Mr Barton said, was demonstrated and more than hinted at, with some modification the scheme would be, ere long, revived, and placed upon a tangible basis. Since the Hull, South and West Junction Railway scheme was thrown out by the stupid committee of the House of Lords, all the portions of the proposed and now temporarily abandoned railway south of the Humber have been re-surveyed, with the undoubted object of presenting in a future session of Parliament a more matured and yet less costly scheme, which while it would utilise the best portions of existing railways, and present new sources of traffic for development, would also present the travelling public with advantages entirely before unknown. It is a well-known fact, that the present systems of railways adjacent to the great centres of industry and population are scarcely equal to the demands of traffic ordinarily presented at the different stations, and at such a thing as a fair or an extraordinarily busy market, the traffic is blocked for an entire day, for at the last Partney fair thousands of sheep were detained from Friday 18th to Saturday 19th September, making a journey from the Lincolnshire loop-line, at Firsby to Wakefield, last 48 hours. Instances of this kind of neglect might be greatly multiplied but it would only be piling on the agony, and not to much purpose; but sufficient has been said to show how inadequate is the present railway accommodation to public requirements. Lastly, with the immense deposits of iron-stone in Lincolnshire, which is daily being moved, and other large fields of operation waiting only the remote chances, I fear, of better railway accommodation till the public with a dogged determination set about in earnest the task of showing the Legislature that the commerce and enterprise of the country are too important to be entirely placed at the mercy of the railway magnates, whose policy in the future will be like that in the past, based on a selfish regard to individual interest, to the neglect of the great principles of commercial progress and the welfare of the community at large."' (Stamford Mercury, 23 October 1874)

In this speech is addressed the urgent need for further development of the existing railways in the light of accommodating not only the present demands, but also those of the future. There is also interesting personal criticism of the railway companies and the workings of Parliamentary committees.

Contending for the travelling public

In the speech quoted above, there was brief reference to 'presenting the travelling public with advantages entirely before unknown'. This leads us to yet another issue that arose during the months immediately preceding the start of the Kettering to Manton line. While previously the prime concern of the various railway companies had been competing with each other for commercial business, the 'Travelling Public' now emerged as a powerful economic prize to be wooed and won. On 6 June 1874, the same day that it published the proceedings of the Parliamentary Select Committee considered earlier, the *Grantham Journal* reported on another weapon in the Midland Railway's armoury against its competitors, which set off another round of battles in a war that was to continue for several months. The aim was to entice by all possible means passengers from one company to another. The press not only provides fascinating glimpses into the lengths to which the rivals were prepared to go, but also shows how valued had become the support of the travelling public. Here are excerpts from the article:

'PULLMAN CARS: Commenced public running on Monday on the Midland system, between London, Bradford and the intervening towns. Several parties, in semi-quiet nooks, whiled away the time with a rubber at whist – a quiet rubber, it may be noted. The construction of the cars precludes the noise of the wheels. Conversation can be enjoyed as if the parties were seated in a veritable drawing room, instead of being hurled through space at 50mph. On the return journey to the North the luxuries of the sleeping car can be enjoyed. Arriving at St Pancras just before midnight, they have only to enter their apartment and go quietly to sleep, and unconsciously perform the journey to Bradford, where the train arrives at 5.50am. The intervening stations at which places may be secured for the through journey are Leeds,

Sheffield, Chesterfield, Derby, Trent, Leicester, Bedford, and Kentish Town.'

On 10 October the Midland launched another broadside; the proposed abolition of 2nd Class carriages, and this was reported in the press, with the additional information that the company had also decided to charge uniform rates of 1½d a mile for 1st Class passengers, and 1d a mile for those in 3rd Class. It would appear that this decision was not wholly unanimous, for on 31 October, *The Railway News* declared: '...after stating that the Midland Railway Directors have decided to persevere with their scheme to abolish the second-class carriages, they say they have also decided to abide by this decision, and to resign if it should be negated by the shareholders.' Clearly the Directors had moved ahead without consulting the shareholders. On 6 November 1874 the *Stamford Mercury* explained the issues further:

'RAILWAY TRAVELLING – The policy of the Midland railway directors with respect to the abolition of second-class carriage, was severely criticised at a meeting of shareholders held in Manchester on Friday. A resolution was passed, declaring that the step which had just been taken by the Board called for prompt and energetic action on the part of the proprietors, and a committee was appointed to communicate with the shareholders in other parts of the country – THE TIMES says that the Midland scheme is something quite different from what it has been represented to be. Pullman's cars have lately been introduced on the Midland line, and first-class passengers have the privilege of using them on a payment of a slight addition to their fare. The Midland has thus at present four distinct classes of carriages, and if the second-class is abolished, there will still remain three...'

The article continued, and put the arguments for and against the Midland's proposals in great detail, and *The Railway News* said the other companies would adopt a modification of the Midland plan.

During the course of that month urgent meetings were called. On 17 November a large gathering of Midland Railway shareholders was held at Derby to discuss the proposed abolition of the 2nd Class fare and reduction of those of the 1st Class. Mr Ellis, the Chairman, defended the action of the Board, while Mr Hobson moved a resolution approving it and opposing delay. Mr Baines moved an amendment urging postponement of the question and consultation with other companies. After a lengthy discussion the original motion was carried by a large majority. While the Midland itself was in turmoil, other leading companies joined forces against its initiatives. The Directors of the Midland Company announced that they had decided to carry out their scheme but would be glad to confer with the other companies upon any details that may affect their convenience and that of the public.

The Great Northern for one was not deterred. A few days later it produced its own secret weapon, and employed a subversive tactic against the Midland at the same time. This was duly reported by the *Stamford Mercury* and the *Grantham Journal* on 28 November 1874:

'THE GREAT NORTHERN RAILWAY – A London correspondent says: I learn from the Northern Railway Company, that they are preparing an important attraction for the northern express which leaves Kings Cross at 5 o'clock. It will consist of a handsome saloon, in which dinner will be served en route. About twenty years ago the competition between this company and the Midland led to a reduction of fares to so small a limit that passengers were brought from Yorkshire to London and back for half-a-crown. If the recent policy of the Midland should lead to a similar procedure, the Great Northern will, at any rate, have one advantage in being able to offer their customers a gratuitous dinner. This will bring as much custom as abolishing the second class carriage.'

The Midland immediately retaliated. On 12 December the correspondent for the *Bradford Observer* 'understood' that the Midland Railway Company, in view of the fact that 2nd Class ticket holders will be disenfranchised under the new arrangements, had decided to issue 3rd Class season tickets. It was probable that there would be a reduction in the fares for 1st Class season ticket holders. Great concern was instantly experienced by the directors of the other leading companies, and only 12 days later came the report that the Great Western Railway was to join the other companies in reducing its fares to a competing point with the Midland, and that it would also issue 3rd Class season tickets. By 2 January 1875 the situation was so intense that not only did an all-out price war break out, but the leading companies vied with each other to introduce luxurious amenities, such as foot-warmers, cushioned seats, and carpets.

Finally, on 1 May 1875, when the building of the Kettering to Manton railway was about to commence, almost by way of a last salvo in the inter-company rivalry for passengers, the Manchester, Sheffield & Lincolnshire Railway announced to the press that it was making great efforts to neutralise, if possible, the pre-eminence of the Midland in the matter of accommodation for the travelling public. The latest effort in this direction was the production of several improved carriages that would either be used as special family saloons, or run in the best fast trains between Manchester or Liverpool and London.

Of the four leading railway companies discussed throughout this chapter, we now consider only one: the Midland. From small beginnings in 1832, the company was formed by amalgamation in 1844. By the 1870s it had progressed to become, according to mileage, the third largest railway company in Great Britain. Despite its name, its interests were not confined to the Midland region. During those 30 years it had concerned itself with building new lines, and its network extended north, south, east and west. Its locomotives travelled the land, and its steamships crossed the Bristol Channel, the Irish Sea and the English Channel. By the mid-1870s it had pushed its own line right into London, and the colossal work of building St Pancras station was nearing completion. At this time also, intent upon opening up country where formerly no railway existed, its territory was extended ever further northwards, to cross seemingly impossible terrain, by the building of one of the most famous stretches of line in the kingdom, the Settle & Carlisle Railway. Seventy-two miles long, the first sod was cut in November 1869; it was opened for freight in 1875, and for passengers in 1876, and thus was contemporary with the building of the Kettering to Manton line.

The Kettering to Manton railway, then, was not a little local scheme to be built in isolation. It was planned to be a vital component in the Midland Railway's overall plan to have its own main line 'from the gates of Scotland right into the heart of the capital' independent of all other companies. To recapitulate, the project was to create a route direct from Nottingham and the great central coalfield to Kettering, well placed in the iron-bearing belt. To accomplish this, two new lines, connected by the Syston to Peterborough branch of the Midland Railway, were to be built in conjunction with each other. From Nottingham, one section was to be built as far as Melton Mowbray, where it would run on to the Syston to Peterborough as far as the south side of Manton Tunnel. The other new line – the Kettering to Manton – was to strike almost due south from there for nearly 16 miles, across very difficult countryside, to join the trunk line to London. Though very expensive, there were many advantages to this proposal. The iron-ore fields and the coal deposits would be directly connected. Nottingham had formerly not been on the main line at all, its access being at Trent, some 8 miles away. The time-consuming bottlenecks referred to earlier would be avoided. Most importantly, greater efficiency would be obtained for the ever heavier and longer freight trains by the improved gradients of the new line.

So, with its position as an important link in the Midland Company's national scheme, and its geographic location connecting the iron and coal deposits both with each other and the important industrial centres, the promoters of the Kettering to Manton railway were well justified in moving forward. The Royal Assent was obtained, the route was agreed, the shareholders contacted, the finances raised, and the surveys completed. Despite the enormous difficulties expected and the consequent financial burden, the work was authorised to commence.

3
THE WORK BEGINS

It is a country of high breezy uplands, divided by wide river valleys. The River Welland makes its leisurely way west to east through richly cultivated districts, from Sibbertoft to the Wash. For 34 miles the river marks the county boundary between Leicestershire, Rutland and Northamptonshire, winding through boulder clays between escarpments of limestone and ironstone, the tableland rising steeply to 300 feet or so on the Northamptonshire side. Beyond that towards Kettering, the River Ise and Harpers Brook also flow from west to east towards the Nene. Though these rivers are insignificant for most of the year, they are subject to floods, and while there have been many years of drainage schemes and flood prevention in the interests of modern arable farming, in certain conditions the Welland can still become half a mile wide. This was even more the case when the railway was being built. To the north of the Welland, on the Rutland side, are set small rural communities and scattered farms, and the rivers Chater and Gwash are but tiny streams flowing east through their wide valleys. The villages have grown very little since the 1870s; more land is arable now, the fields are larger and there are fewer hedgerows, but otherwise the scene is much as it was when the railway people arrived in 1875. To the south, up on the Northamptonshire ridge and beyond, however, it is all very different.

The extraction of iron-ore over a wide area has now completely obliterated almost everything the navvies would have recognised. How Corby, then a remote village in Rockingham Forest, became the centre of the steel industry and grew and developed until in the 1950s it was designated as a New Town, is the subject of other books. Corby town is still expanding. Though the steel industry has mostly gone, and open-cast mining for the iron-ore has long since ceased, the effect on the Northamptonshire landscape through which the line passes has been changed for ever from the richly wooded and gentle slopes as described by Barrett.

This then, is the landscape through which the railway was to be built. It was to cross the 'grain of the country', Barrett's phrase, a point that cannot be too much emphasised, and the key to why this was the most difficult topography with which the railway engineers had to contend in the Eastern region. When building the railway along the desired course and maintaining the gradients to the required levels, tunnels had to be bored, hillsides traversed, immense quantities of earth and rock shifted, and millions of bricks made and laid. Therefore the work was costly in finance, manpower, and heavy equipment. To cross the Welland valley alone would need two tunnels on either side of what was to become, and is to this day, the most obvious and dramatic feature of the whole line, the Welland Viaduct. There were to be other tunnels, and other viaducts, cuttings and embankments, all to build a railway over the comparatively modest distance of less than 16 miles. Despite the high cost, the Midland Railway Company was authorised to go forward, and the contracting company was Messrs Lucas & Aird.

The Kettering to Manton line: some statistics

Length	15½ miles
Cuttings	16
Embankments	12
Viaducts	5
Tunnels	4
Surveyors	C. B. Baker and Crawford Barlow, 1875
Contractors	Lucas & Aird, London
Work started	July 1875
Works completed	July 1879
Equipment and supplies, as reported by Barrett	
Locomotives	17
Portable and stationary engines	56
Pumping engine	1
Horses	120
Bricks	90 million
Lime	9,000 tons

Surveys, legal requirements and landowners

However, before the manpower and equipment arrived to actually start the construction, much preparatory work had to be done. The firm of Barlow, Son & Baker, civil engineers for the Midland Railway Company, was commissioned to undertake the survey for the new line. As Williams wrote:

'The difficulties which arise in planning the course of a railway are sometimes great. The engineer has to visit the districts through which the line may pass, and perhaps make a selection from three or four eligible routes. Trial shafts and borings are made by the assistants of the engineer, which reveal the geological formation of the various strata, and which may present important facts which will have to be regarded. Having completed his observations, and collected the information of his assistants, the engineer sums up the evidence, and marks out the route which the line shall take. Rivers and streams are crossed as near their source as possible, hills and valleys are skirted, and a general estimate is made for setting off the amount of cuttings or embankments as nearly as possible against one another. The route of the line must now be surveyed and levelled with the utmost precision.

A representation is made on paper, and also a delineation of the slopes of the hills, as the whole would appear if projected on a horizontal plane. The ground has also to be levelled in order that it may be ascertained how much higher or lower is any given point on the surface of the earth from any other. The engineer is thus able to adopt measures for reducing the whole of the new line to a level, or to such gradients as may be deemed most expedient to adopt.' (From F. S. Williams, *Our Iron Roads*)

The civil engineers carried out the work in the spring and early summer of 1875. From their recommendations the plans were drawn, and the course laid out. As expected, it was found that even the 'most expeditious route' would entail great difficulties and expense.

Williams tells us that once the surveys for a projected line were completed, the documents had to be deposited with the clerks of the peace of the counties through which the line was to pass, and also with the parochial and other authorities. Every landowner received a section plan showing the depth of cutting or embankment on his estate. The principal landowners in the case of the Kettering to Manton line were the Duke of Buccleuch, the Marquess of Exeter, Lady Cardigan, Lord Lonsdale, Lord Winchelsea, Sir W. de Capell-Brooke, the Hon W. C. Evans-Freke, Colonel Tryon, Rev Charles Boys, E. P. Monkton, W. Shields, and W. C. Thornhill, some of whom we will meet again elsewhere in the book. As Williams said: '…only after all this has been settled, can the petitions be transmuted into an act of parliament; and thus the subscribers are authorised to incorporate a company … and are provided with the powers requisite for their work.'

Machinery and personnel arrive

In June 1875, within weeks of the completion of the survey, the contractors dispatched by rail from other works heavy machinery and other equipment into the district, as close as possible to where it would be used. This was a great strain on the transit resources of the local railway stations where it was all off-loaded and held. Then it all had to be transported to and assembled on the various sites before construction could begin. Portable and stationary steam engines, pumps, locomotives, wagons, gearing equipment for the tunnel shafts, mortar pans and so on were brought in day after day. The congestion caused by so much traffic was tremendous in this remote and isolated district. We can but imagine the confusion as huge machinery was hauled along narrow country roads, then dragged through mud and mire across the fields to the works location. Reports in the local press were sparse, but one did record lanes being blocked, as up to 18 pairs of contractors' horses, each pair with its own handler, struggled to take a single locomotive on a wagon several miles from the nearest station to the works; and there was at least one instance when it took three days to convey such an engine 5 miles. Williams described such an operation:

'To take so weighty an affair as a locomotive along a common road is not a trifling matter, especially if the distances it has to travel are considerable, and hills intervene. Then may the old turnpike-roads be seen invaded by a team of sixteen or eighteen contractor's horses, each pair under the guidance of an appointed driver; while the gleaming brass-work, the black funnel, and the metal ribs of the engine, form a striking contrast to the rural simplicity and tranquillity that stretch around.'

(A hundred or so years later a similar event occurred, when a massive dragline 'walked' under its own power from the open-cast ironstone mines at Exton in Rutland, to the Northamptonshire ridge between Gretton and Corby. It rejoiced under the name of 'Sundew', and as hedges were flattened and road surfaces were protected, notices all along the route proclaimed: 'Excuse me, I'm walking to Corby'.)

The contractors also brought in a nucleus of personnel to achieve the preliminary work of assembling the equipment. According to Barrett, the heavy plant brought to the works included 17 locomotives and 56 portable and stationary steam engines varying from 6 to 20 horsepower; a total of 73 items. He said there were 26 mortar pans, most of which were working day and night for many months. A single pumping engine worked above Glaston Tunnel for three years, and pumped 6,700 gallons every 12 hours, or about 4,891,000 gallons of water annually. The water pumped out of the workings by means of this engine, he wrote, supplied all that was needed within a radius of one mile, quite a consideration when we remember that so much machinery on site was powered by steam. Scores of trucks, trolleys and wagons were brought to the works. There were 120 railway horses, highly trained to the specialised work, while a large number were also hired locally, as required, for general haulage.

It may perhaps be noticed that there is not a mechanical excavator of any sort included in the list above. Joseph Ruston's 'steam navvy' had been invented, and indeed was first employed in this country during the construction of the Midland line from Nottingham to Melton Mowbray, which we remember was the Kettering to Manton's 'sister line'. The navvies themselves did not like the new machines, although they did not present so much of a threat to their jobs as may be supposed. While the steam-powered machines dug out the 'muck' more speedily and cheaply than the men could, they were limited in their use, for they left near vertical sides to what had been cut out, and an army of men still had to follow along behind to trim back the cutting slopes, or they would soon fall in. In addition, the steam excavators were unstable and were the cause of accidents, one of which happened during the building of the Seaton to Wansford line.

Above Annie is on the contractors' temporary way during the building of the Great Central Railway in the mid-1890s. Notice the typically wide age range of this navvy gang. The usual terrier seems to have gone off somewhere! When the work began, heavy equipment such as this contractors' locomotive was taken to the nearest station on an existing line, then hauled overland by teams of horses to where it was to be used. *Newton Collection, courtesy of the Record Office for Leicestershire, Leicester and Rutland*

Below Stationary engines also had be got to site, as this one providing power for a mortar mill on the Great Central works. *Newton Collection, courtesy of the Record Office for Leicestershire, Leicester and Rutland*

This was reported in the *Stamford Mercury* in September 1877:

'Kings Cliffe – a frightful accident occurred on the new railway near Cliffe last week. As the men were engaged in working the ponderous machinery called the "steam navvy", the principal chain used in winding up the scoop gave way, and caught a man employed underneath, cutting open his body and causing his bowels to protrude. He was carried to a neighbouring shanty, and now lies in a very precarious state, no hope being entertained of his recovery.'

The report on the inquest appeared the following week:

'Mr Parker, coroner, held an inquest on the 20th at the shanty on the new line of railway, in the parish of Blatherwyke, on the body of R. Morton, a navvy from Manchester, who was fatally injured on the 13th while working the steam navvy. He lingered until the 18th. Verdict: accidental death.'

In 1894, when the Great Central Railway was being driven southwards towards London, 43 of the 'mechanical monsters' were employed. The Kettering to Manton was probably the last major railway construction to be built entirely by manpower.

Huts erected and workforce arrives

All along the course huts were erected where the greater part of the workforce was to live; these settlements and their locations will be described later, in Chapter 5. The contractors housed the hut families first, who took in several unmarried men as lodgers. Many hundreds more took lodgings in the villages adjacent to the line. Barrett supplies a very graphic description of the arrival of the main workforce:

'By and by the platforms at Manton, Seaton, Rockingham, and other local stations, began, as some of the much-vexed station masters could tell you, to present a very busy and sometimes perplexing scene. Navvies, with their wives and families, might be seen standing in little knots discussing the route, or crowding round the officials asking their way to the new line. Huge bundles of bedding, boxes of household stuff, sundry articles of furniture of all kinds, bedsteads, frying-pans, bird-cages, perambulators, clocks, chairs, and other things too numerous to mention, arrived by every train.'

Hundreds came to the works on foot. As the word went up and down the land that work was to be had, men came tramping into the district from all parts of the country. Singly or in groups and gangs, these men presented a fearsome appearance, hung about as they were with bedrolls, picks and shovels, mugs and saucepans, lanterns and beer jugs, and even in some cases with wheelbarrows strapped to their backs. These were the type of navvies the locals had come to dread. They were the wild ones, constantly on the move, and whose collective bad reputation had gone before them.

Administration

As soon as the heavy equipment was on location, the hut settlements erected, and the men were assembled, the work commenced along the whole length of the line. Messrs Lucas & Aird of London were at that time the main contractors for the Midland Railway Company and carried the work throughout.

Mr James Eagle was appointed by Lucas & Aird as their local agent, responsible for the whole contract. He had come from Germany to manage these works, and was to superintend the whole of the construction until the spring of 1877, when he went to Egypt to take up a large contract there. Meanwhile his daughter had married into a Gretton family, and on his retirement Mr Eagle returned to the village. He became a Gretton parish councillor and was largely responsible for introducing oil street lighting in the village, lit for the first time on Christmas Eve 1895. Sadly he died the day before, and he and his wife are both buried

Once started, the work commenced along the whole length of the line, and soon 'a very ugly scratch was drawn across the face of the country', as seen here on the Great Central. *Newton Collection, courtesy of the Record Office for Leicestershire, Leicester and Rutland*

at Gretton, a handsome headstone marking their grave. His descendants live in the district still. Mr Eagle was succeeded by Mr R. Stannard, who then supervised the works until completion.

The course was divided into four districts, and company agents were in charge of these, with independence of action but responsible first to Mr Eagle and later Mr Stannard. Mr C. J. Wills was in charge of the section north and south of Glaston; for Seaton, Messrs Clegg, Hughes and Wills; for Corby, Mr White; and for Rushton; Messrs Roberts and Blue. Under these were the clerks, the time-keepers, inspectors, subcontractors, foremen, gangers, store-keepers, etc, and a 'host of others all rendering valuable aid in carrying out the scheme' (Barrett).

No time was lost, and the work began in 1875, the same year that the survey had been made. Most of the earthworks were completed in 1878, and the Welland Viaduct in 1879. At the end of that year both new sections from Kettering to Nottingham were opened for freight traffic, thus proving their safety. A few months later the Kettering to Manton line was carrying the Scottish express.

Gretton, as the central village, was the location of the chief engineering office, with a staff of clerks and draughtsmen under Mr A. C. Priestley AICE. Here also was the cashiers office, at first under Mr William Thompson, later Mr T. G. Jones. Gretton was also the centre for the engineers of the company, represented by Mr Crawford Barlow CE, partner in the abovementioned firm of civil engineers. Mr Barlow had representatives at key positions all along the works, who had independent authority but were ultimately responsible to him.

I did not find anything in the newspapers about the start of the new railway works, as there probably would be today. Neither were there reports of any official ceremony to mark the beginning of the project, such as 'the breaking of the first sod', although Barrett made a passing reference to an unofficial gesture at Rushton crossroads, at the southern end of the works. However, the *Stamford Mercury* of 13 August 1875 published:

Men, shovels, picks and barrows begin to change the landscape for ever. Notice the 'gaffer' with his bowler hat.
Newton Collection, courtesy of the Record Office for Leicestershire, Leicester and Rutland

'KETTERING – the new line of railway between Rushton and Manton has commenced. Messrs Lucas and Aird are the contractors, and their headquarters are at Kettering. These works, together with the line being constructed between Kettering and Cransley, cause the town to be unusually busy. The staple trade therefore is in a flourishing condition.'

Since the 'staple trade' was the manufacture of boots and shoes, the arrival of thousands of extra pairs of feet in the neighbourhood clearly brought a considerable boost to the industry. An article in the *Grantham Journal* of 23 October 1875 included: 'The number of bricks required for the viaduct on the Midland Company's line at Seaton is estimated at 26,000,000, and they are to be made on the spot'. We will look further into the effect on trade and industry in Chapter 5.

Thus the course was staked out and fenced, and the contractors' lines, or 'temporary ways' put into place, along which the materials and spoil were to be moved. The first important work began with the sinking of a deep shaft near what was then Corby Wood. This was the beginning of the construction of Corby Tunnel, which had to be completed and operational before certain other sections of the works could commence (see Chapter 6). Along the 15 or so miles the various sections were let to subcontractors, who took on the cuttings, bridges, excavations, road arches, etc. Since the work proceeded simultaneously, in a very few months hillsides were hollowed, masses of brickwork was built, piles of clay appeared over the tunnels, and 'a great scratch was drawn across the face of the countryside'. Along the rough temporary ironways, steam engines drew truckloads of timber, coal, lime, powder, bricks and other materials. The work progressed day and night. 'Who can forget the scene at night,' wrote Barrett, 'with watch-fires glaring far and near in the darkness … the glare of the forge …the flickering lamps of the workmen and watchers as they passed up and down on their respective errands…'

Traces still remain: original railway fence, Midland Railway boundary markers, and the remains of a telegraph pole. *Author*

4
THE NAVVIES

Manpower was the prime energy source in the building of the great public works of the Victorian era. The navvies were thus unquestionably essential to the economy of the nation. Yet they were a despised and feared class. Their mysterious, gypsy-like nature, the isolation, the very independence, was regarded as alien, and therefore invited prejudice. Perhaps a present-day parallel may be drawn from the prospect of the arrival of 'new age travellers' into a district – people of a different life-style and unconventional behaviour, with no obvious roots, whose very appearance tends to evoke hostility. A legacy from the age of canal building was their reputation for drunkenness, riotous behaviour and lawlessness, which went before the navvies wherever they were – a reputation, it must be said, that was not without justification, as police reports testify. On many occasions there was violent opposition to the navvies coming into a district. This was particularly so when the first railways were thrust through the countryside. Certain landed gentry in well-documented cases put the hunt, the game, and even the rabbits before the men, and refused to allow them to lodge with their cottagers, or contractors to erect huts near the works. An example of prejudicial attitude was recorded some time before the Kettering to Manton line was due to commence. An accident occurred on a railway works, and in answer to a query regarding casualties, the reply was that there were so many men injured, so many horses and a few navvies, the implication being that navvies were not only considered less than men, but were less than animals – indeed,

were classed as brutes. Mothers, it was said, threatened their children that they would be given to the navvies if they did not behave...

Hard-working and indispensable though the railway navvies undoubtedly were, landowners and villagers alike viewed their coming with suspicion and fear. There was a very good reason for this. The navvies were different. In a society where thousands of the labouring classes were bound either to the factory bench or to the tied agricultural cottage, here was a class at liberty to roam the land at will, an option open to very few. The navvies also had the reputation of being independent of spirit. Several writers of the time imply that they were more intelligent than others of the labouring classes. Through constantly moving from place to place, their experience was wider, and perhaps their wandering life did not promote the in-breeding that so often attended more settled but insular communities. Both Mrs Garnett, who devoted her life to missionary work among the navvies, and Rev D. W. Barrett, made the point that they were even outside the tyrannies of the Poor Laws, since these were practically inoperative for this group of people. If he was ill-treated, or merely wanted a change, Mrs Garnett wrote, the navvy was prepared to tramp vast distances. She cited an example of navvies from Kent tramping all the way to Westmorland for an extra fourpence a day. On the whole then, the navvies differed from the typical agricultural labourer, mechanic, mill-hand and collier, for their life, though isolated, was free.

Wherever a new construction was to be built, the navvies descended in hordes, and

'A navvy on the tramp': a cartoon of 1855. *Author's collection*

alarm was often raised against them by certain people of status and influence. For example, in his diary of 1838, a Middlesex clergyman, one Rev B. J. Armstrong, wrote: 'The railway spread dissatisfaction and immorality among the poor, the place being inundated with worthless and overpaid navigators...' Another example is this fragment from a book written and published by Lieutenant Peter Lecount, an assistant engineer in the employ of Robert Stephenson, someone, it must be said, whose own living depended upon the navvies. 'These banditti,' he wrote, 'are generally the terror of the surrounding country; they are as completely in a class by themselves as the Gypsies. Possessed of all the daring recklessness of the Smuggler, without any of his redeeming qualities, their ferocious behaviour can only be equalled by the brutality of their language...'

It was necessary for surveyors and civil engineers to enter private land in order to carry out their work, prior to the presentation of proposed routes before Parliament. When landowners objected to the encroachment of railway work, forces of gamekeepers, estate workers, and even hired thugs were frequently rallied to prevent entry to their estates. In the

press, many cases of serious altercations between surveying parties and landowners were reported. Large bodies of men were mustered to protect those doing the initial work, and the navvies, of course, readily took part in the defence of the surveyors and civil engineers. From the navvies' point of view, there was not only the enticing prospect of a free-for-all, but the project, when successful, ensured employment. A very famous and much-quoted example took place in November 1844, less than 12 miles from Manton as the crow flies – the 'Battle of Saxby Bridge'. One of the most determined struggles of its kind, it arose through one privileged person's hostility to the advance of a railway, in this case the Syston and Peterborough line.

The navvies arrive

Thirty years later another body of strong and determined men were gathering. However, when the navvies came to construct the Kettering to Manton line, they were numbered not in hundreds but in thousands. Although by the 1870s the building of a railway was not automatically attended by the spontaneous scenes of violence that had horrified and appalled whole populations in earlier times, there was always the possibility. Experiences such as those quoted would still be fresh in the minds of many. Moreover, other lines as well as the Kettering to Manton were either under construction or about to begin. One of these, the line between Seaton and Wansford, was already in progress. A note in the margin of the Seaton Baptismal Register in January 1876 records: 'There are now about 35 huts built of wood for the accommodation of the Workmen employed by Messrs Lucas and Aird, the Contractors for the Midland Railway Company. Messrs Moss, Contractors for the Seaton and Wansford line, had about 10 huts for their men at the same time.' So for a while there were two lots of navvies working for two different contractors on two different lines, based at Seaton. Although I have found no evidence of conflict between them, it is understandable that parishioners would feel themselves under threat.

By the autumn of 1875, great numbers of railway people had assembled, with many more arriving daily. On 23 October the *Grantham Journal* carried this report:

'The navvies at the new railway works in Rutland are causing much anxiety to the more timid portion of the inhabitants of the district (indeed the very word "navvy" seems to be quite a bugbear). Those who thus regard them would find, if they visited their huts, that although they are extremely rough in manner, they are as a rule good-hearted fellows, who are by no means unapproachable by those who can find a kindly word for them. They have, however, no respect for the provision of the Game Laws, considering, as they say, that "game is made for those as can catch it". In consequence of this prevailing conviction, gentlemen who have hitherto preserved their game are shooting it down as rapidly as possible.'

Several interesting points are raised here, not the least the matter of the Game Laws. However, contrary to received opinion, navvies in this article are put forward as 'good-hearted fellows' who respond to a kindly word. But it was not always possible for the navvies to mix easily with the resident population, kindly word or no, for although many did take lodgings in neighbouring villages, the greater number stayed in the hut encampments, closer to their work but considerable distances from the populated areas. However, as the work progressed on the Kettering to Manton line, there were to be many social opportunities for interaction between the railway people and the local communities (see Chapter 10).

Who were the navvies?

But who were the navvies? What did they look like, and why indeed were they called 'navvies' at all? We can do no better than to consult the much-quoted Victorian writer, Frederick S. Williams, for his is the definitive voice of Victorian railway history. In *Our Iron Roads*, first published in 1852, he wrote:

'The word "Navvie" is an abridgement of "navigator", a class of men first employed in the construction of the canals that immediately preceded the railway era. Many were "bankers" from the lowlands of Lincolnshire and Cambridgeshire, where they had made the banks and cut the canals by which waste lands were recovered from marsh and sea. The wages offered by the railway contractors drew great numbers from the hills of Lancashire and Yorkshire, and they had the boldest characteristics of the Anglo-Saxon stock. Their great strength, their knowledge of embanking, boring, and well-sinking, and their familiarity with the nature of clays and rocks, gave them special qualifications for making railway earthworks.'

Strictly speaking, then, the word was originally used for those employed in the excavation by hand of unimaginable tons of material during the construction of canals and drainage schemes. It soon came to be applied to any man engaged in the building of all kinds of public works, no matter what his trade or skill, and that is the context in which I use it. However, of the men themselves who worked on the Kettering to Manton railway, I have found only a very small number who actually referred to themselves as navvies (see below). Williams continued with this description:

'The "navvie" of the period wandered from one place to another. He usually wore a white felt hat with the brim turned up, a velveteen or jean square-tailed coat, a scarlet plush waistcoat, with little black spots, and a bright coloured 'kerchief round his Herculean neck, when, as often happened, it was not left entirely bare. His corduroy breeches were retained in position by a leathern strap round the waist, and were tied and buttoned at the knee, displaying beneath a solid calf and foot encased in strong high-laced boots.'

Thus he painted a possibly romantic word-picture of the navvies of an earlier era. The

Great Central navvy groups outside their hut, and having a bread and cheese break on a summer's day. Again, the ages range upwards from the lad in the foreground above, and the ubiquitous terrier dog takes pride of place. *Newton Collection, courtesy of the Record Office for Leicestershire, Leicester and Rutland*

jaunty 'dandy' navvies must also have still been present on the Kettering to Manton line as late as the 1870s, for Barrett mentioned that although boots and shoes and other necessary items of clothing were expensive, some navvies contrived to spend 10 shillings on silver-topped walking sticks! Several writers of the time refer to the navvies as fine figures of men, which was no doubt attributable not only to the physical outdoor nature of their work, but also to their diet, far more nutritious than that of others of the labouring classes, and their wages were higher too.

Where did they come from?

The phrase 'armies of navvies roaming the countryside' is often used by railway historians, giving from a modern point of view the erroneous impression of a nationally organised mobilisation of forces. But contractors did not order, as generals on a battle-field, vast companies to be moved to the scene of the next major civil engineering project, although nucleus workforces were retained and deployed for that purpose. Mrs Garnett wrote of the 'great nomadic tribe of tens of thousands' tramping from one end of the country to the other, but stressed the freedom of movement already touched upon. The men were constantly on the move, either from one public works to another or to different parts of the same construction on which they were working. They may be 'on the works' for a short time only, or for several years. But even those employed on the one line for any length of time did not necessarily stay in the same place, but moved along as the line progressed.

Information gleaned from parish registers shows that many of the men employed on the Kettering to Manton line either brought their families with them, or married local women. However, as the railway was built between 1875 and 1879, the construction fell between census years. Thus this important source of personal information regarding names, families, ages, occupations and origins for the majority of the workforce has never existed. However, after the line became operational a minimal workforce was retained in some of the parishes, and thus appear in the 1881 Census, and from these it is possible to gain some insight into their lives. For instance, five railway families were still at Seaton in 1881, and continued to be employed by Lucas & Aird. The Enumeration District for Seaton reads: 'Seaton Parish. The whole of the Parish of Seaton including the Railway Station, Brick Yard, Royces Mill and Seaton Lodge. There are also remaining at the present time four of the huts which are occupied by persons employed by Messrs Lucas and Aird in the construction of the Manton and Kettering Railway', and these we will look at later.

In spite of the myth that still prevails suggesting that 'they were all Irish, weren't they?', only a handful of obviously Irish names are recorded in parish registers and newspaper reports. When the work on the Kettering to Manton line was at its height, it was estimated that more than 4,000 men were employed, though only a comparatively small number appear in local records. Those who do, however, prove how far many of the railway people had travelled before they found themselves in this part of the kingdom. The man who allegedly had come the farthest was one Robert Mills, who was fined for being 'drunk and riotous' at Uppingham on 19 August 1876. He claimed he was from North America, or so the newspaper report had it. No official works records were kept of the manpower, for most of the men were employed on a temporary basis, and foremen and gangers did their own hiring and firing. Not all of those employed on the works came from far away, though from the registers and press I found the greater number working on the Kettering and Manton line originated in distant regions: Buckinghamshire, Cambridgeshire, Cheshire, Cornwall, Devon, Essex, Gloucestershire, Huntingdonshire, Kent, Lancashire, Middlesex, Northumberland, Staffordshire, Westmorland, Wiltshire, Worcestershire and Yorkshire.

Many of the miners came from Wales, originally to bore the tunnels. This is obvious from the surnames, though very few Welsh place names or counties occur in parish records. In most cases the registers, police reports, etc, only refer to 'North Wales' or

Mr Boon, believed to have worked on the Gretton section: this studio portrait is the only photograph received to date of a navvy of the Kettering to Manton workforce. *Courtesy of Gerald Boon*

in the hut settlement at Wing crossroads during the construction of Wing Tunnel. According to a contemporary report, they spoke amongst themselves in Welsh, and their English had such a strong lilt that there was much mutual confusion between them and local people, as must have happened between the Enumeration Clerk and John Price in 1881.

John Price was a Welsh railwayman living with his family in Wing village at the time of the 1881 Census, and the entry is shown below. At first glance he appears to have brought his wife and eldest daughter with him when he came to work on the tunnel, but on reflection there is more to the entry than that. There is not a Guildfield in Wales, though there is a Guilsfield not far from Welshpool. The only Duddington is in Northampton-shire, significantly within a couple of miles of the works on the Seaton to Wansford railway. It is very likely that the railway work brought John to the district, to be employed by Messrs Moss somewhere along the Duddington section of the Seaton to Wansford line. He met and married Hannah, and then took her back to Wales. Leighton, where Elizabeth was born, is very close to Guilsfield, John's birthplace. Meanwhile, many Welshmen had come to work for Lucas & Aird on the tunnel at Wing, almost within sight of Hannah's home village. It is possible she was homesick, and since there was still plenty of railway work to be had, John brought her and little Elizabeth from Wales to Rutland, probably in 1877. They lived at first in the hut settlement at Wing crossroads, close to the works on the tunnel. There Matilda was born. When the work on Wing Tunnel came to an end the family moved into Wing village, and by 1880 their third daughter, Emily, was born. The

'South Wales', probably because the dialects led to communication problems. The spelling skills of the local clerks were in any case precarious, and the complicated place names of Wales would not help. Many of the navvies could not spell either (see below). Quite a colony of Welshmen and their families lived

The Price family

Name	Status	Age	Occupation	Birthplace
John Price	Head	36	R/way labourer	Montgomery, Guildfield
Hannah P	Wife	32		Montgomery, Duddington
Elizabeth P	Daughter	6		Montgomery, Leighton
Matilda P	Daughter	3		Rutland, Wing
Emily P	Daughter	1		Rutland, Wing

Kettering to Manton line was finished and operational when the census was taken, but John was still employed by Lucas & Aird.

Not all of those employed on the works had travelled far distances. Many came from the neighbouring counties of Leicestershire, Lincolnshire, Northamptonshire and Rutland, and a considerable part of the workforce was made up from the villages along the course of the line, for the registers show 'employed by Lucas and Aird' or 'employed by the Midland Railway Company' when referring to local men. In the 1870s Depression with a capital 'D' visited agriculture in this region as it did elsewhere, and farm labourers were frequently taken on for short-term work, and found welcome alternative employment. They could lead a horse or fill and wheel a barrow as well as the next man, and there were many other menial jobs that could be done by casual workers. But it was the specialist navvies that did the toughest and most dangerous work.

Three families were recorded on the Seaton Census return as living in 'The Railway Contractor's Field', and two were living in the village itself. Presumably the fourth hut mentioned above was unoccupied on Census Day. As we look at these families, some of the points raised in this chapter are highlighted.

Below are details of the Ackland family. The birthplaces of this family give an excellent example of the wandering life already discussed. Spare a thought for Thomas's wife, Charlotte. In 14 years she had borne seven living children, moved five times, and still lived in a temporary home, one of the huts that remained on the 'Railway Contractor's Field' at Seaton. Amy Louise was baptised at Seaton on 25 January 1880, when Thomas's occupation was given as 'Railway Clerke'. He will appear elsewhere in this book.

Also below is the Douglas family; Mr Douglas was evidently not at home on Census Day. Here we have an example of movement within the works. On the day of the Census this family were neighbours of the Acklands in the huts at Seaton. But three years earlier they were living at the railway huts at Glaston. On 31 January 1878 Francis Anne Lambert, daughter of William and Isabella Douglas, was baptised at Glaston by Rev D. W. Barrett. William's occupation then was given as foreman fitter. They moved along the line to Gretton, where Rose was born, and by 1881 had crossed back over the valley to Seaton,

The Ackland family

Name	Status	Age	Occupation	Birthplace
Thomas Ackland	Head	42	R/Storekeeper	Kent, Lewisham
Charlotte A	Wife	38		Essex, Hatfield
Charlotte A	Daughter	14		M/sex, Whitechapel
Herbert A	Son	11		Essex, Walthamstow
Mary A	Daughter	9		M/sex, Clapton
Edith A	Daughter	6		M/sex, Clapton
Mabel A	Daughter	4		Rutland, Lyddington
Alexanda A [sic]	Son	2		Rutland, Lyddington
Amy A	Daughter	1		Rutland, Seaton

The Douglas family

Name	Status	Age	Occupation	Birthplace
Isabella Douglas	Head	34	Engineer's wife	Durham, Uswork
Francis D	Daughter	3		Rutland, Glaston
Rose D	Daughter	10 mths		Northants, Gretton
John Lambert	Nephew	18	Portable engine	Northumberland, Newcastle driver
Eliza Smith	Servant	15	General servant	Yorkshire, Dalton

and had gained a lodger. Their nephew John had come to live with them, as had Eliza Smith, the daughter of another railway family who had been on the works. Eliza may have chosen to stay on with the Douglas family when her own people moved away. Perhaps she and John had become interested in each other. Note that Francis's third given name is Lambert; possibly Isabella's maiden name and certainly nephew John's surname. I could not find Uswork in County Durham, but there may be a confusion here because of a conflict with Isabella's Durham accent – probably as obscure as the Welsh to the clerk at Seaton. It is possible that she could not write the place name herself (see below). William was not at home on the day of the Census, so we do not know where he was born, though Isabella and John both come from the North East. We see from the Census that Isabella is given as an engineer's wife. Three years earlier, as we saw, William's occupation was registered as foreman fitter.

We now have a much-travelled household, the Smith family (see panel opposite). Mr Smith the engine driver was also not at home, so we do not know his Christian name, though it was probably John, since that is the oldest son's name; neither do we know his birthplace. It is unlikely that Eliza Smith, the 15-year-old general servant living in the Douglas's hut, was of this family. We see that Mary, aged 12, was given her mother's name, as was frequently the case with the eldest daughter. We can but imagine the hard life of this railway wife. In 12 years she had seven living children, and since the eldest was born she had moved at least six times. As well as a husband and seven children to care for in the crowded hut, there were also three unmarried male lodgers. A hard life indeed, and she was still only 38 years old. Alongside the two Barrow-in-Furness birthplaces is the note 'on the tunnel'. One wonders how much schooling the little scholars had been able to absorb as they were moved from place to place. Upton Pyne is in Devon, so there is an understandable clerical error here. I could not find Soltforth in Yorkshire, but there is Salterforth. There is a mystery about another locality, Beadwell in Derbyshire. There is a

Beadnell in Northumberland, a Beadlam in Yorkshire, a Bednall in Warwickshire… Look at the birthplace of 27-year-old James Beard – Settle in Yorkshire.

The Shaw and Simmons families (see panel opposite) were living in the village at the time of the Census. We can deduce that the Shaw family had lived for at least four years roughly 10 miles from where Abraham was born, for Sutton Bassett, locally abbreviated to Sutton, is close to Market Harborough, but across the River Welland in Northamptonshire; here then is an example of the employment of a local man on the railway. Did Abraham go to work in Yorkshire, meet Jane there, then bring her back to the new railway works? Or did Jane perhaps come to Sutton 'in service'?

The Simmons family give an example of a railwayman marrying into the local community and settling down. From the Seaton Marriage and Baptismal Registers we learn some details. William Simmons, bachelor, of full age, was married on 1 January 1878 by Rev Thomas Heycock to Ella (sic) Smith, also of full age. William's occupation was given as a miner, so it is likely that he had come to Seaton to work on the tunnel. He must have been a first-generation railway worker, for his father, Elias, was a farm bailiff, presumably in Devon, where William was born. Ellen was the daughter of Thomas Smith, labourer, of Seaton, and George and Kate Smith were the witnesses to the wedding. Both William and Ellen signed the register with a good clear hand, while George and Kate's signatures were not so fluent. William did not move on after the tunnel was finished, as many of the miners did, for he has appeared in the Census Return. Robert William, the 1-year-old son, was baptised on 29 June 1879 by Rev Thomas Heycock. Here his father's occupation is given as Railway Labourer, so though the tunnel is finished he continues his employment with the railway.

Both William and Ellen could write well, but many of the railwaymen and their brides either signed with a cross, followed by someone else countersigning 'his/her mark', or they signed themselves with so shaky a hand that one feels it was about all they could manage. On 17 August 1877 the *Stamford*

The Smith family

Name	Status	Age	Occupation	Birthplace
Mary Smith	Engine driver's wife	38		Devonshire, Uptonpyne
Mary A	Daughter	12	Scholar	Lancashire, Withnell
Emily	Daughter	11	Scholar	Yorkshire, Soltforth
John	Son	8	Scholar	Yorkshire, Freeston
Louisa	Daughter	6	Scholar	Lancashire, Barrow-in Furness
William	Son	5	Scholar	Lancashire, Barrow-in Furness
Ada	Daughter	4		Derbyshire, Beadwell
Thomas	Son	1		Rutland, Seaton
James Roberts	Unmarried man	50	General labourer	Gloucestershire, Stroud
William Wilson	Unmarried man	30	Railway engine driver	Gloucestershire, Cheltenham
James Beard	Unmarried man	27	Railway engine driver	Yorkshire, Settle

The Shaw family

Name	Status	Age	Occupation	Birthplace
Abraham Shaw	Head	30	R/Platelayer	Northants, Sutton
Jane S	Wife	31		Yorks, Rotherham
Elizabeth S	Daughter	4		Rutland, Seaton
John S	Son	1		Rutland Seaton

The Simmons family

Name	Status	Age	Occupation	Birthplace
William Simmons	Head	33	R/labourer	Devon, Wadland
Ellen S	Wife	26		Rutland, Seaton
Robert William S	Son	1		Rutland, Seaton
Alice S	Daughter	4 mths		Rutland, Seaton
George S	Brother-in-law	22	Permanent-way labourer	Gloucestershire, Willesby

Mercury published an extract from an article entitled 'The Ebb and Flow of Life', in which is included these statistics regarding the 139 marriages that had been celebrated in Rutland:

'15 men and 14 women signed the register with marks. In 8 cases both parties signed, in 13 only one. The percentage of men who thus signed is small – 10.8% – Rutland being one of the 9 counties in which the proportion of men who thus confessed their ignorance is low. The proportion of women is also low, 10.1%... Of the 619 births, 18 male and 21 female were illegitimate... Rutland stands at the head of those counties in which there was a striking increase in the rate of these births.'

We could speculate on the effect that the sudden influx of all those comparatively well-off and possibly glamorous strangers might have had on village maidens...

Miners such as William Simmons would have worked from a shaft like this on the Great Central. Similar scenes would have been seen above Corby and Glaston Tunnels. *Newton Collection, courtesy of the Record Office for Leicestershire, Leicester and Rutland*

Thus were gathered the men to build the new railway. Some stayed only a day or two, others for several years. Some came with their families and worldly possessions, others with their gang of mates and their tools, many came tramping in to the works alone, with only what they stood up in. The navvies had come, but, as Terry Coleman wrote, '…they must never be confused with the rabble of steady, common labourers, whom they out-worked, out-drank, out-rioted, and despised. A navvy was not a mere labourer, though a labourer might become a navvy.' (*The Railway Navvies*) Some left their names behind in church registers, in newspapers, or criminal records. Records show that of those who married into local families and settled down, many of their descendants live there still. Many, far too many, railway workers lie in unmarked graves in village churchyards, as indeed do railway women and children, victims of accidents, illness and childbirth. But at least one young navvy's name is recorded on his lonely grave, though I have yet to find out how he died. In a hidden corner of a Northamptonshire churchyard, tucked away under some trees by the wall, is a stone bearing the following inscription:

IN
MEMORY Of
WILLIAM THOMAS WINFIELD
WHO WAS KILLED ON THE
KETTERING AND MANTON
RAILWAY
IN COURSE OF CONSTRUCTION
OCTOBER 8TH 1877
AGED 29 YEARS.

ERECTED BY HIS FELLOW WORKMEN

'BOAST NOT THYSELF FOR
TOMORROW: FOR
THOU KNOWEST NOT
WHAT A DAY MAY
BRING FORTH'.

The greatest part of the workforce went away when the work was done, as anonymously as they had arrived. Some of the local men who found employment on the works went away too, to follow the call of the wandering life, though most of them returned to their rural occupations. Some of the local women went also, having married into the navvy life. But the railway remains to this day, as silent witness to the men who built it.

5
THE SETTLEMENTS AND HUT LIFE

Directly the work was under way, men arrived daily in great numbers from all parts of the country, and went along the course until they found lodgings and employment. As we have seen, some came by train in gangs, some came tramping to the works in ones and twos. Many brought their wives and families. Many more were single men. Think of the effect all this must have had on the people in these remote and isolated villages. This was, and to a certain extent still is, a rural and sparsely populated district. Strangers, even singly, had always been noted and regarded with suspicion. Now they came in their hundreds; strangers with the reputation of wildness, drunkenness and lawless behaviour going before them. Whether deserved or not, it was the character that was ascribed to the navvies. Like many generalisations it was not necessarily correct. Few of the railway workers called themselves 'navvies' or were so described in the parish records and newspaper reports. They had many different trades and skills, as we will see in the next chapter, and most were hard-working, decent men. But a gang of men who worked on the railway would be considered as navvies by the villagers no matter what their work was. These communities and their resources were overwhelmed and were threatened by the sheer numbers. We will look into this more fully in a later chapter.

Lodgings in the villages

A group or 'gang' of railway workers who followed the same trade or hailed from the same place tended to travel and live together.

Navvy accommodation	
Huts	205
Rushton	26
Corby Wood	50
Gretton	12
Glaston	70
Seaton	47
Housing, men	1,500
women	307
children	700

Hundreds took lodgings with local families living in the villages and outlying farms close to the works. Many villagers not only took in lodgers – a useful boost to income – but many local men also picked up temporary employment. Indeed, much of the unskilled labour force was drawn from the local villages, and some of these men moved on with the navvies when the work was done. On the other hand many navvies married local girls and settled down, and some of their descendants live in the district still. It was estimated that up to 1,500 men either lodged or lived in the villages, and walked to the works daily. In most cases the living conditions for these lodgers were very crowded. For example, at Seaton a certain public house was lodgings for workers on the viaduct. The lady publican slept them 12 to a room, and it is said that she had to keep her liquor always securely locked up. This establishment was then called the Three

Horseshoes. It closed in 1955, and is now known as Croft House. We must remember that living conditions for the labouring classes at that time were crowded anyway, and by the standards of today intolerably so. The Company also rented accommodation for the staff on a more formal basis in almost every village, when rooms and whole houses were taken up by the contractors. This applied particularly to Gretton, where, as the central village of the line, the main engineering office with its staff of clerks and draftsmen was located.

Contractor's settlements and locations

However, the majority of the workforce lived along the line. Lucas & Aird erected temporary settlements at sites where the railway people were concentrated in the greatest number for the longest time. For example, 400 men were employed at the great viaduct and its brickworks for more than two years, so there was a contractor's settlement of 47 at Seaton. The construction of Corby Tunnel took more than four years, for this was a key element in the line, as we saw elsewhere. There were 50 huts in Corby parish to house over a thousand men working at the tunnel and the cuttings on either side. In the Glaston district there were 70, at two sites either side

of the tunnel. At Gretton there were 12, and near Rushton 26. For a short time there was also a group at Wing. As Rev Barrett pointed out, if all the 205 contractor's huts on the Kettering to Manton works were put together with a space of 20 to 30 feet between, they would form the equivalent of a street about 2 miles long. The resident population in these settlements, excluding those living in the 'shants', was estimated at being in the region of 2,500. In addition there were great numbers of women and children. I know I labour the point, but we must be aware that there was constant movement of this population, either from one works to another or a different part of the same line. When the work was at its height it was estimated that about 4,000 men were employed along the whole works. Imagine then the impact on this rural district, where four years earlier the 1871 Census records that in the 58 parishes of Rutland the total population for the whole county was 22,073. Across the Welland the Northamptonshire villages along the route were just as sparsely populated.

Typically, the contractor's settlements consisted of rows of standard wooden huts, which usually measured 24 feet by 16 feet. Some modern writers refer to these as 'shanties', but this is not how the Victorian authors wrote of them, as we will see below. As like as not the navvies and their wives had

Part of an engraving from *Life and Work Among the Navvies* shows the settlement at Seaton yard. It was estimated that 400 men were employed on the viaduct and the brickworks, which is to the left.

been born into the life – had been born in a hut and had lived in several places already before coming to work on the Kettering to Manton line. A foreman and his family would rent a hut, and his gang lodged with them. This was an arrangement much favoured by the contractors, for it gave an element of stability to the workforce. There were three rooms in the contractor's huts, a general living room and two sleeping places, one for the use of the family and the other for the lodgers. This room was always crowded, for there could be as many as 10 to 20 men lodging there. It was furnished with rough beds and a few boxes and shelves. I could not imagine how so many men could be fitted into such a small space, having seen some of the huts that still survive. Then I came across a reference to 'sleeping in the manner of immigrant ships', which I took to mean bunks one on top of another. The family sleeping room in the best huts was more comfortable, and the general living room would have a long table, a couple of forms and a few chairs, etc.

The huts had to be equipped with up to a dozen beds and blankets, cooking utensils and crockery, washtubs, containers for water, and so on. The men all washed out of doors, and much of the cooking and washing was done outside, for these were wooden buildings, well tarred against the weather, so would be a real fire hazard. Large fires were necessary not only for cooking but to dry the men's clothes after a day's work in the cold and wet. I have found only one reference to accident by fire in the press, which we will see later. Barrett gives glowing descriptions of some of these huts, and although this was a transient population, some families did stay for the full four years, so some of the huts were real homes, with a 'bit of garden, a few fowls, and a pig'. The rents were payable to the contractors. As well as those rented by families, sometimes a hut was taken on by a gang of single men, who installed one or two women to cook and clean for them. These were frequently rowdy households, subject to fights breaking out. Other huts were rented by women, some of whom were railway widows.

There were also in the contractor's settlements two larger buildings. These were the store, where everything could be bought, and the 'shant', where strong beer was sold and which housed the men who tramped in to the works for a day or two, then tramped out again. The 'shants' will be considered later. Some of the contractor's huts, incredibly, still exist, though not on site. Aware of the temporary nature of the settlements, Barrett recorded for posterity their locations: 'Many who take up this book will be glad to see a record of their exact locality, for by the time this reaches the reader's eye, they will, in all probability, be swept away…' And swept away they were, even before his book was published, leaving hardly a trace of the busy communities that had dwelt in them. To use his words:

'Coming from Manton Station, and travelling towards Kettering, you will have passed groups of them opposite the Chater Viaduct, on Wing cross-roads, along the valley to the tunnel, and on Glaston hillside. Seaton hill was crowned with a cluster known as "Cyprus". In the Welland Valley on the Seaton side was another settlement. Some few were scattered all along by Gretton; on the borders of Corby Wood was quite a Canadian forest scene in the busy camp that was formed there. Smaller lots were erected at Penn Green, Thorny Lane, Harper's Brook, and the crossroads at Rushton.'

The comparison with a Canadian forest scene was not as fanciful as it might at first appear. Barrett was writing in 1879, the West was being won, the Indian Wars were being fought, and Custer had had his last stand. Pioneers were forging their way into new territories – and as the railways and those who were building them advanced further and further westwards, they brought with them development, progress and civilisation. Wherever railways were constructed, there were the navvies and their encampments. So when Barrett wrote somewhat romantically of 'the little colonies as they crown the hills, cluster down the slopes of the undulating ground, or nestle in the valleys and woods half hidden by trees…', his was indisputably our

Above This navvy hut stood in Arnhill Road, Gretton, until it was demolished to make way for a garage in 1993. Built in the 1870s, it is said that it was used as an office by the railway contractors. *Arthur and Elisabeth Jordan*

Left This navvy hut still stands by the Seaton Road at Glaston. When these pictures were taken in 1992 the hut was in a sorry state and looked as if it would not survive another winter, but it was good to see recently that it is now in good order. The hut is reputed to have been the chapel, but I cannot confirm this. *Author*

This hut is at Gretton, and was photographed in the early 1990s. Though it is still there it has since been much altered. *Author*

authentic eye-witness account, but he made no mention of the dreadful weather, or the mud, or the misery.

Navvy huts and shelters

On railway works there were often several miles between established lodgings and where the men were employed. Small gangs took on contracts for a few days or weeks, perhaps while constructing a farm access to land soon to be divided by the line, or a conduit for a stream to pass beneath, and such employment was remote from the main sections. Therefore in addition to the accommodation provided by Lucas & Aird, and that found in the villages and outlying farms, all along the works were clusters of rough huts made by the men themselves, and here too families lived. Barrett said that some of these huts were of rough stone roofed with tarred boards, others of boards roofed with branches and bracken. Some were woven wattles, plastered with mud and thatched with straw. Some were of sods of

earth, and others merely holes in the bank, lined with whatever came to hand. He remarked:

'They grew like mushrooms ... taking your stand on any one point of the line above ground, I do not think there was a single spot from which you could not see a hut, or the smoke of it anyhow, rising from one of the little chimneys and curling up in faint blue wreaths from some snug nook, where the humble home was hidden by a dip in the landscape.'

The reference to 'one point above ground' alludes to the fact that so much of the line was built through tunnels.

But Mrs Garnett was far less romantic, much more realistic. Her depictions were probably much closer to the mark, and her experience was very similar to Barrett's. She said the worst shelters were not fit to kennel dogs in, with rain dripping through rotten felt, damp penetrating the sides, and fungus growing on earthen floors. Towards the end of a contract repairs were neglected. The winters were terrible in those years, as we will see, and eye-witnesses wrote of icicles a foot long hanging from the roofs.

Conditions compared with Stamford

Awful as these conditions were, they were by no means worse than some endured by others of the labouring classes of the time, whether in the slums and tenements of the industrial cities or the tied farm cottages of the less enlightened landowners. An article in the *Stamford Mercury* of 12 January 1877 illustrates this. A report of the monthly meeting of the Sanitary Committee of the Stamford local Board includes:

'Spencer's Terrace, Stamford: Most of the houses visited by Mr Battle, found them with one or two exceptions, horrid dens, some of the rooms not more than six feet high, and most of the places being in a filthy, dilapidated tumble-down state. In one place a man, his wife, and six children all lived in one room, the only other place being uninhabitable even for those poor creatures. In his opinion the tenements were totally unfit for human habitation, and decidedly injurious to health. Besides this, on the terrace were a cluster of closets from which foul and horrid stenches were constantly emitted. He felt sure that if an official inspection of these houses were made by the proper parties the places would be at once condemned as unfit for habitation, and he moved that the medical officer of health and the surveyor be instructed to inspect the terrace and report to the next monthly meeting of the committee – seconded by Mr Thompson and carried...'

That was not all. The article continued. Alderman Wright observed that there were many other houses in the town equally as uninhabitable as those in Spencer's Terrace.

Mr Howard said he was quite aware of the state of the houses in the terrace, and that there were many other places in the town equally bad; but if such places were closed, where, he asked, were the inhabitants of such places to go? He was reminded that that was not a question for the Board...

At least the navvies and their families had fresh air, and were not trapped for a lifetime in a squalid tenement. But they were isolated, and lonely, and worked long hours in exposed situations. I know from my own experience how bleak the region can be, when the east wind is channelled through the valleys direct from Russia, or the west wind brings driving rain, with nothing to break the force of it. And so the men made their primitive huts, to live in for a short time, and built small sheds as shelter against the weather beside their work. It was said that the making of shelters was as instinctive to the navvy as nest building is to a bird.

The 'shants' or 'shanties'

The English language is constantly evolving. New words enter the language, others drop out of use, and still others change their meaning entirely, as has 'navvy', or 'navvie': a corruption of 'navigator', which originally referred to those employed on the building of canals – the inland navigation. Then it came to be applied to the pick-and-shovel brigade of the early railway builders, and by the 1870s it was universal terminology for anyone engaged on public works. It is clear when reading contemporary accounts that the word 'shanty' has not the same connotation now as it had then. Today we would most likely ascribe the words 'shanty town' to any collection of ramshackle dwellings – indeed, such as those discussed throughout this chapter. But originally, in the sense of how the phrase would be understood in the 19th century, the 'shanty system' was a debasing and demoralising feature most often associated with navvy life.

Both Mr Barrett and Mrs Garnett employ the word 'shant'. 'Shants' were classed as far inferior accommodation, and had acquired a very bad reputation. Those that lived in them do not appear in statistics, other than by implication. Structures of wood and felt, the walls were tarred or whitewashed. Of varying size, they were larger than the standard huts. The shanty-keepers were often described as unscrupulous, and in a situation where overcrowding was the norm, the 'shants' were overcrowded to a disgraceful degree. There are accounts of 'shants' built to accommodate 80 men being crammed with 120. Shanty-keepers charged a halfpenny for men to sleep on the floor, a penny to sleep on a table, and fourpence to sleep on a bed.

In addition to the problems of overcrowding, strong drink was sold, which of course brought its own problems. The 'shants' were notorious for the drunken state of the men, and for the fights that ensued as a consequence. The men who had to resort to the 'shants' for their lodging were most likely the single isolated men, who were constantly 'on the tramp'. Men without roots or ties, often addicted to the travelling life, they wandered anonymously into a works for a day or two, then drifted on. Drink no doubt brought welcome oblivion for such men, for as Mrs Garnett said, the loneliness of the wandering life was dreadful, yet the freedom of being 'on the road' was fascinating. Cold, hungry and tired, a man on the tramp had every temptation to drink, for it was available. Many 'shants' were not erected by contractors on railway land at all, but put up close by as unofficial lodgings by enterprising but possibly unscrupulous individuals, eager to take advantage of the situation. I have not found an example of this on the Kettering to Manton line.

The 'shants' in the settlements along the Kettering to Manton route were set up by the contractors, and the shanty-keepers were regarded as respectable men. However, frequent incidents occurred, fights broke out, and drunken scenes reminiscent to us of those depicted in 'westerns' were briefly mentioned in the press. On 18 March 1876 the *Grantham Journal* report on the proceedings of the Rutland Assizes included the case of John White, alias Ginger, railway worker employed by Lucas & Aird on the new railway works at Seaton. He was charged with stealing from the person of George Williams. This crime affords us, in the words of the *Journal*, an interesting glimpse into the 'shant' at Seaton one winters' night:

'George Williams, the prosecutor, said he was a navvy working on the railway at Seaton, and lodged at a "shant" or shed kept by Thomas Oxenham. On the night of 26th February, between the hours of 9 and 10, he went to his lodging and on going to bed found it occupied by another person. He went to the living room of the "shant" where was the prisoner and four others. He sat down near the stove, and shortly after the prisoner began pulling him about, upon which he told him to let him alone. He had in his pocket two tobacco boxes, and one florin, six shillings, 1 penny and 1 half-pence [just over 8 shillings, more than a day's wage]. The penny was a new one. The money was in one of the boxes. Afterwards he went to sleep, and when he awoke, found his pocket had been cut off and the monies [sic] stolen. He accused the prisoner the next morning of stealing them. Charles Morris, navvy, said on the 26th February he was in the same room with the prosecutor and prisoner. He saw him take the money out of the tobacco box, and then throw it on the floor; he afterwards told the landlord what had taken place. Thomas Oxenham said he kept the "Shant" at Seaton to accommodate 40 men. The prisoner and the prosecutor lodged there. On the evening of 26th February, the prisoner paid for his lodgings and other things, and told the witness he was spent out. The next morning he heard Williams accuse the prisoner of stealing the money, amongst which the prosecutor said there was a new penny. On the same day the prisoner came to the witness for some things, and brought a florin and a new penny. He then communicated the robbery to the police. The prisoner, who has no witness, said he neither cut Williams' pocket or took the money...'

John 'Ginger' White was found guilty and sentenced to three months imprisonment with hard labour. In Chapter 11 we will see what sentences like this meant.

The 'shant' system at its worst was an exploitation of human beings whose strength and endurance was the key element in the great engineering achievements of the Victorian era. At its best, however, when well regulated by responsible contractors, such as Lucas & Aird, it was a very necessary means of lodging extra men when they had to be taken on for a project that might last only a few weeks, and for the wandering population who roamed new works seeking casual work.

Women on the works

Mrs Garnett said that just as the navvies were different from others of the labouring classes, so were the navvy women. Theirs was a strange life, she said. Living in many different parts of the country, they probably did not look on anywhere as home. They were used to the hard work. If they had been born in a hut, they were accustomed from childhood to living under the same roof with 10 or 15 lodgers, as well as big brothers. They were noted as having a free and masterful manner. They were mostly ignorant and untaught, married early, and probably took on a hut near their mother, and so the life went on.

But imagine preparing meals and cooking for 10 or 15 men out of doors over an open fire day after day, month after month. Imagine cleaning up after them all, making a dozen beds, washing and dressing the children, washing the men's clothes, all without the benefit of electricity or running water. Imagine being either pregnant or recovering from childbirth most of your fertile life. Imagine giving birth over and over again in a crowded hut with only a neighbour to act as midwife. Imagine the illnesses you would have to cope with, the accidents, the deaths. And on top of all this and more, imagine never having a permanent home, moving on where your man's work took him, leaving friends you had made and with whom you had shared life's crises. But then you had probably been born in a hut yourself, and had known no other life. If

your man was killed on the works, you might be allowed to continue the tenancy of the hut and take in lodgers in your own right, but that would be up to the contractor. If your man had gone off, as many did, you could stay on for two weeks, but after that you would have to find your own rent, find your own way, for you wouldn't go 'on the parish'.

Of course this toil and drudgery was not confined to the navvy women, but it is relevant to emphasise the contrast with how we live today. We take so much of modern life for granted. There is another aspect to consider. Our families are not only small, but we approach the birth of our babies confident that unless something unusually tragic occurs, we will survive their birth and they will survive their childhood. Furthermore, we stand a very good chance of living beyond our fertile years.

Mary Anne Welsh-Moss

Of all the hundreds of women who lived and toiled by the Kettering to Manton works, here we look at just one. When looking through the registers of Seaton parish, one name caught my eye: Mary Anne Welsh-Moss. How unusual I thought, a 'double-barrelled' name. From the Seaton Baptism Register I noted on 31 March 1877, Phoebe Amy, daughter of John and Mary Welsh-Moss, of No 28 Railway Huts, Seaton Yard, was baptised by Rev D. W. Barrett. Her age was not given, but her father's occupation was given as Brickmaker. Thus I concluded he was working at the brickyard connected with the great viaduct. Four months later, on 8 July, two other little girls, also of this family, were baptised. They were Mary Anne Emily, aged three years, and Clara, who was six. I think that although they were registered as daughters of John and Mary Anne Welsh-Moss, John may not have been their father.

From the Marriage Register, we find that two months later, on 2 September 1877, John and Mary Anne were married by Rev Thomas Heycock. They were both of full age. He was a bachelor, a brickburner, of No 22 Midland Railway Huts, and he wrote well. She was given as Mary Anne Moss, also of full age, a widow of

Seaton. She signed with a cross. Their fathers were George Welsh, brickmaker, and James Fletcher, labourer, who also signed with a cross. The witnesses were John Foster, who signed with a cross, and Mary Ann Smithersman, who signed her name. This was the only example of that surname I found. It therefore seems that John worked with his father George making bricks, and Mary Ann née Fletcher was the widow of Mr Moss, who was possibly the father of Mary Anne Emily and Clara.

Five months later Mary Anne was dead. On 3 January 1878 she was buried at Seaton. She was 33 years old.

Pleasures and pastimes

It was not all work and toil, neither was drinking oneself into oblivion the only recreation. In the chapter devoted to the Mission, there are accounts of entertainments that took place at the hut villages. The railway people themselves entertained each other, as this report in the *Stamford Mercury* of 9 March 1878 relates:

'KETTERING AND MANTON RAILWAY WORKS, SEATON DISTRICT – An entertainment, consisting of comic songs, glees, recitations and a hornpipe dance was given on 26th ult. at the carpenter's shop (lent for the purpose by Mr Stannard) … the programme … was gone through in a manner which delighted an audience of about 300 people, chiefly composed of railway workmen, their wives and families. The performers were the employees of Messrs Lucas and Aird, assisted by a few friends. The Rev B. Margetty of Lyddington kindly presided at the piano… The duets of Masters T. and C. Ackland were rendered in a style which showed they had undergone some training in vocal art. The temperance song, by Mr P. Kelly, a total abstainer of long standing, was received with rapturous applause. The hornpipe and war song by Mr Canning simply 'brought down the house', while Mr McClough's recitation (Uncle Ned's Tale) was

listened to amidst the most complete silence, receiving at the end of it well-deserved and hearty recognition… The chair was taken by Mr Bruster, the lay-reader, in the unavoidable absence of the minister, the Rev D. W. Barrett… The proceeds amounted to £9 10s 8d, and will be devoted to the Mission sick fund.'

This was one of many entertainments reported in the press during the railway years. It is not only a delightful glimpse into a pleasant evening, but gives a little more insight into life on the works. We have met Mr Stannard before. The Rev Margetty had come along the valley from Lyddington for the evening to play the piano, and this is the only reference I have found of him by name. It is interesting to note that the railway people had overcome the local prejudice implied in earlier chapters, for outside friends had not only been part of the entertainment, but were also part of the audience. It is also interesting to note that the carpenter's shop was big enough to seat 300 people.

The *Stamford Mercury* detailed the whole programme, which comprised 35 items. At first I thought Mr Kelly, surely an Irishman, was one of the foremen, but later I found him when he appeared with Mr Barrett on the top table when the viaduct banquet took place, so I now believe him to be one of the unnamed lay-readers. We will meet Mr Canning and Mr Bruster again. The two young Masters Ackland, if they were the sons of Thomas, whom we met on Census Day, may have moved away when the Census took place, for it does not record boys with the initials T or C. But 'T' could stand for Thomas, and the first son was often named after his father, so I speculate that they were of this family. Glees were unaccompanied part songs, like barber's shop quartets. The sum raised for the sick fund was considerable.

In the better weather men enjoyed out-door pursuits; kicking a ball about or roaming the hedgerows with their dogs, to the consternation of the local gamekeepers. Some lived on the works long enough to have a bit of garden. They wandered into Oakham, Uppingham and Kettering as well as the neighbouring villages. In April 1876 Sanger's Circus was in the district. The newspapers reported that when it visited Uppingham, it was attended by great numbers of people:

> '...the navvies of the district mustering in full force. A serious accident was with difficulty averted, when a large van containing eagles, vultures, and other exotic creatures would have overturned in the street, but a number of these men rushed up just in time to prop up the vehicle with their strong arms...'

As the settlements became established, reading rooms were provided, and there are accounts of little groups of men with their pipes sitting in the warm as they listened to one of their number who could read, or playing cards and draughts. Surprisingly, for men whose work was hard and physical, they must have been nimble with their fingers, for I have read that they were clever at carving, and made their own trousers, shirts, and slops. Slops? I didn't know either, but a slop is a sort of smock, and also slops are baggy trousers.

Sarah Ann Bloomfield

Hundreds of children came to live in the huts and were born in the huts. Many of them died in the huts too, either in infancy or of childhood illness, the only record of their short lives being a stark entry in a parish register. Some, however, met with a tragic accident. From an inquest report I have gleaned the sad story of a dreadful day in the life of a young mother, Caroline Bloomfield.

Caroline was married to Arthur, a ganger employed on the works. They had three children, the eldest being Sarah Ann, and they all lived in one of the huts at Cresswell, a settlement near Gretton. On 28 March 1877 the child of one of Caroline's neighbours fell ill. Caroline left her two younger children in the care of Sarah Ann, while she went to see if she could help. She had only been gone a minute when another neighbour, Jane Dixon, rushed in to tell her Sarah was on fire. The flames were put out, and Sarah was able to say that her little brother had put a stick in the grate and then put it on her dress. She had been burned so severely on her abdomen, chest and arms that she died on the following Saturday. Verdict: death from burning. Sarah Ann was four years six months old.

Thus the hundreds of men, women and children arrived and continued to arrive daily, to stay until their work was done or until the call of the wandering life lured them away again. Then they either moved out altogether or along the course to other employment. Drunken behaviour did still take place. There was still violence and crime and disregard for the law of the land, of that there is no denying, but they occurred in any society and any class. The navvies did not hold the monopoly.

6
BUILDING THE LINE

As Rev Barrett wrote: 'There is probably no country line in England in which so much work has been compressed in any equally continuous length. It is much to be compared to the well-known Settle and Carlisle line for difficulties in construction, but has been more costly per mile than even that expensive undertaking.' The contract between Lucas & Aird of London and the Midland Railway was for £650,000, or £41,200 per mile, a huge sum for the day, reflecting as it does the heavy nature of the work.

Now, we are not thinking of moorland and mountainside, bogs and quagmires here, but a few miles of apparently gentle English landscape. Yet the prospect of building this line was considered so fraught with difficulties and consequently so expensive that it was not until the early 1870s that all the legal preliminaries and the necessary funding were obtained, the surveys and planning accomplished, and the work commenced. The phrase has been quoted that the line had to go 'across the grain' of the country, and we have looked at the countryside over, through, and under which it was to pass. We have also considered that it could only be built at great expense, because of the heavy work. So what did this heavy work entail?

We are looking here at a line on which, to maintain the levels and desired gradients as near as possible to 1 in 200, there are 16 cuttings, 12 embankments, four tunnels and five viaducts. The crossing of the Welland Valley alone involves Corby Tunnel to the south, 1,920 yards long; the viaduct across the valley, which is 1,275 yards long; and Glaston Tunnel to the north, which is 1,842 yards long. Here is a line of which one-fifth, or 3½ miles, is either above ground level on the viaducts, or below ground level in the tunnels. Yet the whole line is but 15¾ miles long.

The land had been purchased from the local landowners at the going rate of £30 per mile. The course had been pegged out, the fences erected, and temporary iron-ways constructed. Along these steam engines and horses drew truck-loads of materials: timber, coal, lime, gunpowder, bricks and anything else that needed to be moved from one site to another. I had imagined that when the work commenced it would start at one end, progress to the other, then stop. Not so! As soon as the hut settlements were erected, the plant assembled and the workforce in place, the work began along the whole length of the line more or less simultaneously. We saw in Chapter 3 how all along the works the various sections were let to sub-contractors.

As well as the major structures that we will look at in some detail, culverts and bridges too numerous to record had to be built, each vital in its own right and each contracted to a foreman and his gang. The bridges are, as Williams says, an important class of railway works. They are erected over or under roads, to cross streams, and for communications between fields. Sometimes 'cattle arches' were built, under which the farmers could drive their flocks and herds. Building bridges had its own technology, difficulties to be overcome, and hundreds of men were employed in their construction.

Above The course is pegged out, the fences erected, the temporary iron-ways constructed, and gantries over the working shafts in place.

Left Individual foremen and their gangs took out contracts for cattle arches and road bridges, culverts, drainage work, and so on. This road bridge is in the valley below Harringworth station. *Author*

The cuttings

In order to maintain the required levels, cuttings led into tunnels and embankments ran on to viaducts. On the Kettering to Manton line the cuttings were dug out of ironstone, clay – blue lias conglomerate and yellow oolitic – and earth. Who regards a cutting or an embankment, all overgrown and hidden by trees and bushes as they are now, with appreciation of the toil and labour that went into their construction all those years ago? Who considers that most of the material dug out was not just dumped on the nearest field, but was moved along the works to form the embankments? Who indeed looks at the embankments anyway? They too have become part of the landscape. Let us see how it was done.

Williams provides us with one of his graphic descriptions of men at work:

'Joining together in a "butty-gang", some ten or twelve of these men would take on a contract to cut out and move so much "dirt", as they denominated the earth cutting, fixing the distance to which it had to be wheeled and tipped. The contract taken, every man put himself to his mettle: if any were found to be skulking, or not putting forth his full working power, he was ejected from the "gang". Their powers of endurance and their consumption of flesh-food were alike enormous. They seemed to disregard danger, and they were as reckless of their earnings as they were of their lives…'

Cuttings claimed lives and serious injuries were received. Men were crushed by falls of earth, or run over by the waggons. The men were paid according to how much 'stuff' was dug out, and were expected to fill 14 waggons a day. Some of the falls were caused deliberately by men undercutting the work to speed up the process. Others were caused by the work altering the natural drainage, and water building up. One of the earliest fatalities reported was in November 1876, when a young man named Palmer, of Geddington, was killed by a fall of earth while working on the cutting near Oakley. He was 19 years of age.

Not all the accidents in the cuttings were fatal. In May 1876 John Munton, of Lyddington, while working on the cutting near Gretton, sustained a compound fracture of his right leg caused by a quantity of earth falling upon him. He was taken to Stamford Hospital. In June John Green sustained serious injuries while working on Seaton cutting. He was unable to avoid an earth slip when several tons of earth fell, which enveloped him. He too was taken to Stamford.

Barrett tells us of some of the quantities dug out of the major cuttings on these works: from Glendon cutting, 260,000 cubic yards, of which about 100,000 was ironstone; from Rushton cutting, 200,000 cubic yards of clay

A cutting leading to a tunnel at Loudwater in the Chilterns in the early years of the 20th century. The photograph gives some idea of how much work was involved in digging out the cutting between Glaston and Wing tunnels. *Newton Collection, courtesy of the Record Office for Leicestershire, Leicester and Rutland*

Left This engraving is from Barrett's book and is worth a few moments' study. It has a lot to say about the digging of a cutting towards a tunnel and the work at the face itself. Near the top can be seen a tip-truck waiting to be drawn up the temporary way, possibly towards an embankment on the other side. Another line leads to the working shaft, down which men and materials would be lowered and spoil drawn up. Two men are standing on a plank over a sheer drop as a lantern is lowered. Others are picking at the hillside and filling barrows, which in turn will fill the tip trucks in the foreground. Over the network of massive planks a man strolls nonchalantly, while another pushes a laden barrow up an incline. Over all stands the 'gaffer' near the middle of the picture. There are also navvy huts.

and stone; and from the cutting south of what was then Corby village, 270,000 cubic yards of clay. Between the village and the south side of Corby Tunnel there is a huge cutting over a mile long and 56 feet deep. From here over half a million cubic yards of earth, clay and ironstone were dug out, more than half of which was run through the tunnel when completed to build the embankment on the

other side. But before the embankment is reached, there is yet another cutting from which 35,000 cubic yards of earth was removed.

Below Gretton village is Cresswell cutting, from which 163,000 cubic yards were dug. Soon after the work on this cutting began, it was found that the hillside was unstable. Several acres near to the village slid down, and all that had been done was lost, so the route was changed further out from the hill, which meant that a different cutting and another embankment had to be made. Then comes Harringworth cutting; Barrett did not record what was dug out here. Across the valley and beyond the Welland Viaduct there is another long cutting divided by Seaton Tunnel, and 150,000 cubic yards was dug out. From Glaston cutting 130,000 cubic yards was removed, from the north side of Glaston Tunnel 55,000 cubic yards, and from both sides of Wing Tunnel a total of 135,000 cubic yards. Most importantly, as far as possible

Looking back along the cutting towards Corby old village from above the south portal of Corby Tunnel. The retaining walls are more than an eighth of a mile long. More than half a million cubic yards of earth and rock were excavated here. *Author*

'stuff' that was dug from the cuttings was transported to where it could be used to form the closest embankment. It was part of the civil engineer's job to devise the most economical use of the spoil.

Why have I spend so long on these quantities? To make the point that every cubic teaspoonful, if there is such a thing, was dug by hundreds of men, not machines. We saw in an earlier chapter that there was not a 'steam navvy' – a mechanical digger – on these works. All the earth, rock and clay was dug by manpower, which is why thousands of men were employed on the line.

So what was expected of these men? This is what Thomas Brassey, the railway engineer of great renown, had to say:

'The labour which a navvy performs exceeds in severity almost any other description of work – a full day's work consists of fourteen sets a day [a set is a number of waggons, in fact a train]. There are two men to a waggon. If a waggon goes out fourteen times, each man has to fill seven waggons in the course of a day. Each waggon contains two and a quarter cubic yards. The result is that each man has to lift nearly twenty tons' weight of earth on a shovel over his head into a waggon. The height of the lifting is six feet. This is taking it at fourteen sets a day, but the navvies contrive to get through sixteen sets … which is not nearly equalled by any other set of workmen in the world.'

Thomas Brassey had employed over 5000 men, and was contractor for the Great Northern Railway, so he certainly spoke from experience.

Another report comes from Thomas Roscoe, a newspaperman, as he watched Brassey's navvies cutting away a hillside:

'By day and night they struggled without relaxing and at night the hill literally swarmed with moving bodies lighted to their work by torches flickering from side to side and from place to place. Creaking cranes, dragging by ropes and pulleys the

laden barrows in their guides and again slowly curbing their descent down the almost perpendicular banks, the clatter of continued footsteps, the heavy sound of spade and pickaxe and busy hum of toiling men completed a scene of unexampled animation.' (Quoted in C. Walker, *Thomas Brassey, Railway Builder*, 1969)

Slave labour?

This was not, as some have implied, slave labour. These railway builders were well paid in comparison with others of the labouring classes. Indeed, one of the reasons for local unrest against them was they were too well paid, and too free with their money, a complaint similarly laid against the American forces during the Second World War – 'overpaid, over-sexed, and over here'.

For some reason, and I have not yet been able to find out why, the work of the railway navvy was considered lighter than the navvies who worked on the docks or reservoirs, yet the wages earned by the railway workers, at 2s 8d to 3s 6d a day, though lower than these, was a big improvement on that paid to those tied to the land or confined to factories. However, the progress of the work was largely governed by the weather, so a piece of work was carried out until, as Mrs Garnett remarked, it was little short of suicide. If the weather was wet, or snow and frost set in, certain work ceased, she said. As you will see in a later chapter, the weather was most severe, yet the line was built and operational in four years – tunnels, cuttings, embankments and viaducts notwithstanding – and according to Barrett the work continued 'by day and by night'.

Breaking down the wages by some of the tradesmen employed on the line, we find that miners earned about £2 a week, though some got much more, according to how tough their work was. The basic rate for bricklayers was £2 10s a week, though again they could earn much more, especially if they worked overtime. Labourers earned £1 to £1 5s, mechanics £1 16s, and the foremen over each class about £3. These wages may not look very much in view of the conditions under which the men worked – the height of the viaducts and embankments, the depth of the tunnels and cuttings, the quantities of 'stuff' shifted and so on, and indeed the conditions in which they lived. But consider that the average weekly wage for men employed on the land in 1870 was less than £1, and for a woman 11 shillings. In that light, the pay was very good indeed. One interesting fact I came across while making these comparisons is that a ploughman walked 11 miles as he ploughed 1 acre of land.

The navvies' diet was far better too. To compare their diet with that of the other labouring classes of the time is to reveal that they did very well. Theirs was tough, hard, physically demanding work, which, as Mrs Garnett wrote, 'necessitated the consumption of most supportive food; good beef, fine wheaten bread, eggs, tea, parsnips etc'. The navvies needed to be well fed, for food was the fuel that fired these 'machines of flesh and blood'. It has been calculated that the diet exceeded 4,000 calories a day. We may find it surprising that in those days of the growing and influential temperance movement, with its battles against the evils of alcohol touched on elsewhere, 'good strong beer' was listed as an important component of the diet.

From studying the parish records and press coverage I have compiled these lists of trades, skills and professions engaged on the works:

Agents; book-keepers; blacksmiths; brickmakers; brickburners; carpenters; centre fixers; contractors; civil engineers; draughtsmen; engine drivers; engineers; excavators; fitters; foremen; gangers; horse handlers; horse keepers; inspectors; labourers; masons; machine men; miners; messengers; night watchmen; painters; plumbers; plate layers; point turners; sawyers; shoe makers; stone cutters; surveyors; supervisors; store keepers; tip boys; time keepers; wheel wrights

Then there were what we might call the true navvies – those who took pride in their work and pride in their strength; those employed because of their skills in embanking, cutting and tunnelling. 'No ganger is needed over them: indeed, they would brook no

'A navvy carrying his dinner': a cartoon of 1855 – not quite what Mrs Garnett had in mind when she wrote of 'good supportive food'! *Author's collection*

Provisions per hut per week

Beer	30 gallons at 3d a pint
Whisky	½ gallon at £1 a gallon
Jam	3lb at 6d a jar
Butter	3lb at ¼d a pound
Sugar	8lb at 5d a pound
Milk	7 quarts at 4d a quart
Ham and bacon	20lb at 8d a pound
Potatoes	5 stone
Bread	20 loaves
Tinned fish	2 tins
Meat	¾lb per person per day at 9d a pound (equivalent to 600 oxen, 3,000 sheep and 150 pigs per year)

supervision ... all that is needed is to see that the levels are right, and to have an engineer to measure the work done every fortnight, against the payday settlement.' (Article in the *Daily News* of 1872) These may have been ordinary men, but their achievement was indeed extraordinary. Yet of all the thousands

Blacksmiths at work during the building of the Great Central line, one of the many skilled trades needed by the contractors. *Newton Collection, courtesy of the Record Office for Leicestershire, Leicester and Rutland*

of men employed on the Kettering to Manton line, I have found very few who were referred to or referred to themselves as navvies. Barrett said that nine navvies out of ten, if asked to describe themselves, would do so in these terms: 'We be fellows as works hard, lives hard, drinks hard, and dies hard.'

The tunnels

There are four tunnels on the Kettering to Manton railway: Corby, 1,926 yards long; Seaton, 206 yards; Glaston, 1,849 yards; and Wing, 353 yards. Just as there was not a steam excavator employed on this line, neither was there mechanical boring equipment. All the mining was done by hand.

In November 1875 the main work of the line actually started with the sinking of a deep shaft at Corby Wood. Corby Tunnel was where the most work was to be done, and this tunnel and the cuttings on either side were to occupy upwards of a thousand men, employed not only as miners, but as brick-makers, bricklayers, blacksmiths, carpenters, fitters, labourers and navvies. The men stayed here for the longest time, and they and their

families were housed in a settlement of 62 huts. Thirty engines of various sorts were used here, and other machinery. The tunnel itself was not only over a mile long, but had to be driven through so that the material from the massive cutting on the south side could be carried through to form the long embankment below Gretton, two miles further north. From this first shaft and nine others the mining took place. The tunnel was built in 423 lengths, and bricked throughout to a thickness of three quarters to one yard, 20 million bricks being used in all. The deepest of the ten shafts was 110 feet; four were bricked down and left as ventilation shafts, and the others were filled in. The tunnel has a span of 25 feet, a height of 22 feet, and has what is known as a 'horseshoe' profile. It is curved towards the north end, and is very wet inside. Its completion allowed other work to commence, for in February 1879 the first trainloads of earth and rubble passed through to form the embankment.

Glaston Tunnel, the second longest on the line, cuts through the high ridge on the north side of the valley, close to the village, and was mined down deep shafts in a similar way to

The view from the north end of Corby Tunnel. There is another cutting with a retaining wall on the east side of the line. *Author*

Corby Tunnel. But it was a more difficult and dangerous undertaking because of the nature of the material through which it was mined: 23,000 cubic feet of timber had to be built into the brickwork, for it could not be withdrawn as was the usual practice. At great expense Staffordshire blue bricks were transported to the site to line much of the tunnel for extra strength. There were also 16 million local bricks used. It was built between 1877 and 1879, and is a straight bore. It also has a span of 25 feet and a height of 22 feet, but in this case the profile is circular. It was not until I walked across the top of the tunnel and saw the great spoil heaps still remaining that I began to realise the magnitude of the work that had gone on so far below.

Glaston Tunnel was not made without incident. On 3 June 1876 the *Grantham Journal* reported:

'A painful rumour (greatly exaggerated, however) got about Uppingham, on Thursday last, to the effect that there had been a frightful collapse in No 3 shaft in the new Glaston tunnel, and that a number of men were buried therein. Considerable excitement was created, but happily this was speedily allayed by the arrival of news to the effect that there had simply been a fall of some scaffolding, which had unfortunately resulted in the dislocation of the ankle joint of one man, and the slight injury of two navvies. Mr Wright was speedily in attendance and recommended the sufferers to the Infirmary at Stamford.'

Mr Wright was one of the foremen at the tunnel. The *Stamford Mercury* also covered this accident, but in less excitable language: nine men were on a scaffold 20 feet high when it gave way, and the men who were upon it fell to the ground. Luckily none were killed. One of them, Charles West, sustained a compound dislocation of the left ankle. The others were not much hurt.

On that same day, also at Glaston Tunnel, a labourer called John Stones fell 130 feet down No 4 shaft. Despite that dreadful drop, he was not killed instantly, but lingered on for several hours before he died. His funeral was held on the following Sunday and was attended by a large number of people.

A year later, in August 1877, No 3 shaft claimed another life, when a 36-year-old married man, John Pickwick, overbalanced and fell the whole 130 feet from top to bottom. Death, not surprisingly, was instantaneous, of a compound fracture of the skull. Mr Shields was the coroner, the jury returned a verdict of accidental death, and handed their fee to the widow.

Above One of Glaston Tunnel's ventilation shafts and a spoil heap, on which stands an ordinance survey triangulation point. The tunnel is to the right. *Author*

Left A close view of one of Glaston Tunnel's four ventilation shafts. *Author*

Below The north portal of Glaston tunnel, and the line's 14th cutting from the south end. *Author*

A few days earlier another fatality occurred at this tunnel, which involved a horse driver, a waggon-load of bricks, and a startled horse. Twenty-six-year-old Frederick Clarke Smith, a single man, was running his horse and waggon into the tunnel at 9 o'clock at night when he was heard to cry out. The brake-man ran to him and found him on the ground unconscious, and before his mates could carry him to the huts he died. It was supposed that the horse had met with some obstruction, plunged, and the deceased was thrown down and trodden on. The inquest was held the next day by Mr Shield of Uppingham: verdict; accidental death.

Seaton Tunnel, at 206 yards, was classed as a short but dangerous tunnel, but I have no other details as to its construction.

Wing Tunnel, although but 353 feet in length, was also difficult to build through the narrow ridge of hills between Preston and Wing village. According to Barrett, here was the heaviest piece of underground work, owing to the great weight of the two over-pressing hills under the slopes of which it had to pass. The valley between them was not shallow enough to allow an open cutting. Initially it was planned to make Wing Tunnel by the 'cut and cover' method, but this was not possible either, because of the pressures. It is partially lined with blue Staffordshire bricks for extra strength, and the brickwork is nearly 3 feet thick all through. There was much rejoicing when it was finished, as we will see in the chapters on the Mission, for despite the difficulty it was accomplished without major incident.

Imagine being lowered in a bucket or basket 110 feet into the bowels of the earth, there to toil for perhaps 12 hours by the light of a candle stuck in a bit of clay, until you are hauled back up again. This method of transporting the tunnel workers up and down the shafts was a precarious business. A report appeared in the press of the death of Jeremiah Downs, aged 37, who received fatal injuries while ascending a shaft in a skep or basket. When he was about halfway up, for some reason or other he fell out

The south portal of Wing Tunnel. The group of buildings on the skyline to the left is Wing Grange, once the home of Mr Brocklebank, a director of the Midland Railway. *Author*

of it to the bottom, a distance of about 109 feet. He received frightful injuries, but lingered on until 2 o'clock the following morning. This death, like many others, was blamed on the victim. The foreman of the shaft gave evidence at the inquest that the deceased had had a drink before the accident took place. Verdict: accidental death.

The viaducts

Although the magnificent viaduct across the Welland valley is without doubt the most visible star of the Kettering to Manton line, there are four other viaducts, not easily seen now unless you are exploring the line on foot. From the Manton end the first is the Chater Viaduct, set across a pretty little valley in Wing Hollow, through which the tiny river Chater flows. It has five 40-foot-span arches, with a rail level of 42 feet above ground. There are railway cottages near here. The nearby meadow near Cromwell Farm was one of the hut sites. Next comes Seaton Viaduct (not to be confused with the Welland Viaduct) between Seaton and Glaston tunnels, under which the Uppingham branch line ran. Seaton Viaduct has eight 30-foot-span arches, with a rail level 38 feet above ground, and is also called Glaston Viaduct. Now comes the famous viaduct across the Welland valley.

Sometimes called the Harringworth Viaduct, sometimes the Welland Viaduct, and sometimes quite wrongly the Seaton Viaduct, it strides for three-quarters of a mile across the valley, visible for miles around. Its 82 40-foot-span arches have an average height of 57 feet at rail level, but 60 feet above ground level at the deepest part. Of the 81 piers, 71 are 6 feet thick and 10 are 12 feet (block piers). How incredible it is to think that this superb structure took only two years and four months to build from start to finish. The fourth viaduct is Harper's Brook Viaduct, or Geddington Viaduct. It has 12 40-foot-span arches, and is 55 feet high in the centre. Finally is the viaduct over the River Ise, near Barford Bridge, which has five arches of 40-foot span and is slightly over 50 feet high.

The viaducts over the River Ise (*below*) and Harper's Brook (*above right*). *Author*

The Welland Viaduct

One of the wonders of the age, indeed still one of the wonders of the country, is the splendid viaduct that carries the line over the Welland Valley. I have found a passing reference to the cost of building being £82,000, but I have not been able to verify this. There are errors in some modern accounts about the viaduct, its construction, and the numbers of men concerned, and myths are thus perpetuated. Let the contemporary press tell the story: on 13 July 1878 the *Grantham Journal* carried this short report:

'THE WELLAND VIADUCT – Lieutenant-Colonel Tryon of Bulwick Hall keyed the last arch to this structure on Friday. The Viaduct is on the Midland Railway branch line from Kettering to Manton, and is one of the longest in England. There are 82 arches of forty feet span, and some are 60 to 70 feet high. The first brick was laid in March 1876, and work will soon be completed.'

Two weeks later there were accounts of the celebrations to mark the event, which Barrett also recorded:

'July 27th 1878, The Welland Viaduct at Seaton – a grand banquet was given by Messrs Lorden and Holmes, the sub-contractors for the Manton and Kettering branch of the Midland Railway on Wednesday evening, the 17th inst., in a large shed tastefully decorated, near the Seaton railway station and above the viaduct, to celebrate the keying of the last of the 82 arches of this magnificent structure. Lieutenant-Colonel Tryon of Bulwick Hall occupied the chair, and was supported by Mr Barlow jnr, Mr Stannard, Mr Brown (surgeon, Uppingham), Mr Orford, Stamford, and about 80 of the engineers, sub-contractors and agents connected with the line. The vice-chair was occupied by the Rev. D. W. Barrett, supported by Mr Brewster, Mr Kelly, etc. The banquet, dessert, wines etc, were supplied by Mr Clifton, of the Crown Hotel, Stamford, which was splendidly served up, and gave great satisfaction.

Above Seaton seen through the arches of the Welland Viaduct; Seaton station, on the Rugby to Peterborough line, can just be seen. To the right and just up the hill is where the celebration for the keying in of the last arch took place. *Author*

Below The arches of the Welland Viaduct present the illusion that they are taller than they really are. Because of the viaduct's great length it is impossible to see more than three straight on, so all the others are foreshortened. Note in this view the 'block piers' that isolate the arches in sets, and prevent any strains being continued indefinitely from arch to arch. *Author*

After the chairman and vice-chairman had proposed the usual loyal and patriotic toasts, Mr Barlow jun (one of the engineers of the line) and Mr Stannard (agent for the contractors) spoke of the viaduct as one of the grandest and most perfect pieces of work in the United Kingdom, and reflecting the great credit upon the sub-contractors, and everyone engaged upon it. Various toasts and songs occupied the evening until twelve o'clock, when all dispersed with three times three cheers for Messrs Lorden and Holmes, for their superb entertainment.'

The following interesting particulars about the viaduct (some of which we know already, but which bear repetition) appeared in *The Builder* of 20 July 1878, and were reproduced by the *Grantham Journal*:

'The Viaduct crosses the Welland Valley from Harringworth to Seaton, in the counties of Northamptonshire and Rutland, and is one of the longest structures of its kind in England, being ¼ mile in length. It has eighty-two arches of forty feet span, some of them 70 feet in height. The eighty-one piers are six feet thick, except ten, which are double thickness, and are called "block piers" to isolate the arches in sets, and prevent any under-strain being continued indefinitely from arch to arch. The average height is fifty-seven feet above ground. The foundations of the piers and abutments are of concrete – some of them are of a considerable depth. The whole of the structure is erected with bricks manufactured on the ground with Derbyshire gritstone springers, string course and coping; the arches and spandrels are all covered with two coats of asphalt. The first brick was laid in March 1876; and the first arch commenced in June 1877. It has been pushed on with such vigour that the arches were finished in the first week of July 1878. The whole of the brick and stone work will be completed by the end of this year or early in the next. The work contains 30,000,000 bricks, 20,000 cubic yards of concrete, and 19,000 cubic feet of stone. Brickwork in lime, 37,543 cubic yards, in cement 5,876 cubic yards. Barrow lime is used in the concrete and mortar throughout the whole work, supplied by Messrs Ellis and Sons, Mount Sorrel Junction, Leicester. Messrs Barlow, Son, and Baker, London, are the engineers for the line, and their inspector of the works is Mr G. W. Smith. The contractors for the whole of the works are Messrs Lucas and Aird, London; their agent on the works is Mr Stannard. Mr Lorden is the sub-contractor for the brickwork, and Mr Holmes is the brickmaker.'

Bricks and brickworks

Think of it: five viaducts with a total of 112 arches, four tunnels bricked throughout, bridges too numerous to recount, drains, culverts and retaining walls, all made of bricks. It has been estimated that 90 million bricks were used during the construction of the line, of which 75 million were made locally.

In July 1875 the *Grantham Journal* reported: 'The number of bricks required for the viaduct on the Midland Company line at Seaton is estimated at 26,000,000 and they are all to be made on the spot.' The brickworks was close to the viaduct, and Barrett's book includes interesting engravings to illustrate this, but no interpretation of what they show.

There was also the brickworks at Uppingham. In 1874 deputations were being made to the Midland Company in connection with bringing the railway into Uppingham, and an article refers to Mr Dean's brickyard. In July 1875 Thomas Nutt, foreman, Uppingham brickyard, had clearly anticipated a boost to the trade, for he placed an advertisement for six good men, accustomed to grinding and serving moulders; also four boys, good wages, wanted at once. Unfortunately Mr Nutt overstretched himself, for the expected trade somehow did not come his way, and he was left with quantities of bricks on his hands. However, as

UPPINGHAM, Rutland.

To *BLACKSMITHS, WHITESMITHS,* and *Others.*

To be LET, with immediate Possession,

A Newly-erected SHOP, situate in the *High-street,* fitted up with every convenience for a Blacksmith's and Whitesmith's Business, and where a good trade has been carried on for many years by the owner. A first-class opportunity is afforded for an energetic steady man, there being a great amount of work carried on in Uppingham and neighbourhood on the construction of Railways, Sewage, and Waterworks. [tion.

The Tools and Stock-in-Trade may be taken at a valua-

For a view apply to Mr. James Sneath, Black Horse Inn, Uppingham ; or to J. Langley and Son, auctioneers and estate agents, Uppingham.

Left The new railway works brought a boost to the local economy – the boot and shoe industry in the Kettering district is an obvious example. Local tradesmen grew prosperous as they brought their goods to the works settlements every pay day. And, as this advertisement from the *Stamford Mercury* of 10 November 1876 shows, the great amount of new work in the area encouraged the expansion of already successful business.

Above and below Two views of brickworks taken from engravings in Barrett's book. Clay is being dug out, trucks are being filled and conveyed to the works, and chimneys are smoking. According to the caption of the second view, the huts are of turf, and in the distance can be seen either Seaton church spire or one of the working shafts.

we can see from the advertisement overleaf, first-class opportunities did occur as a consequence of all the public works in progress in the district.

There was a further brickyard at Gretton, while those at Corby Wood, Corby and Beansfield (also Benesfield and Bainesfield) each produced 100,000 bricks a week. As a consequence of the construction of the railway, the Corby area became a centre for brick-making for a quarter of a century.

Great progress

There was still much work to be done, but great progress had been made until very hard weather in January 1879 almost stopped the work entirely. However, on 22 February 1879 the following account of the report to the Midland Directors at Derby appeared in the press:

'The Kettering and Manton Railway works … the late severe weather has been the cause of considerable delay in the work generally. The tunnels are finished throughout. The viaducts and public road bridges are practically complete, and only a few farm road bridges are needed to finish the bridge work. About 250,000 cubic yards of excavation remain to be removed before completing the earth work. The ballasting, permanent way, and stations are in progress, and the completion of the line may be anticipated in July next. The extensive ballast pits on the Leicester Road have been sold by Mr Willcox, to Messrs Aird and Lucas, the Midland contractors…'

In November 1879 the new Melton and Nottingham section was opened for goods traffic, and on 6 December it was reported the 'new line of railway between Kettering and Manton was opened on Monday morning for goods and mineral traffic. It is expected to be ready for passenger traffic on January 1st, when the work will be fully completed.' Meanwhile, the race continued with the Great Northern, discussed earlier in this book, for on 13 December it was announced that 'The new Great Northern and North Western Railway will be opened on Monday next, from Melton Mowbray to Market Harborough, and by this route it is expected a considerable London traffic will be secured.' Then on 6 March 1880 the *Grantham Journal* reported:

'THE MIDLAND RAILWAY: On Monday last, the 1st of March, the Midland system was further extended by the opening of the Manton and Kettering line for passenger traffic, in connection with the old Leicester and Peterborough line and the new Melton and Nottingham.'

Timetables had been issued, showing a service each way from Kettering to Nottingham, but there was no reported celebration or ceremonial associated with this event. By this time the vast majority of the navvies, their families, goods and chattels were long gone. They went just as they had come, melting away as their section of work was done.

7
THE MISSION

Uppingham Union House (the workhouse) still exists, on the Leicester Road. Architecturally much changed, it is now and has been for many years one of the Uppingham School's boarding houses, known as 'Constables'. There a meeting was called in the early autumn of 1875, under the chairmanship of the Rector of Uppingham, whose name and title was the Chancellor, the Reverend and Worshipful W. Wales, to discuss the first public concern about the large bodies of workmen congregating at intervals all along the course of the new public works – the railway between Manton and Kettering. These newcomers, it was reported, were in danger of overwhelming the existing resources. The various clergy at the meeting, in whose parishes the construction had just begun, declared anxiety as to the effect such masses of people would have upon their flocks. And how could the spiritual and moral provision for the visitors be supplied, when they, the clergy, were already stretched to the limits by the requirements of their own parishioners? Something, the meeting declared, must be done. Urgent though these needs were seen to be, they did not develop into immediate action. A catalyst was needed.

And one appeared. The following spring, the Right Reverend William Connor Magee, Bishop of Peterborough, came to this part of his diocese on a confirmation tour. He stayed at Uppingham and asked to see for himself the progress of the works and the people who had come to build the railway. With his Chancellor, distinguished clergy, and dignitaries associated with the works, he and his wife travelled from Glaston to Manton in ordinary open trucks along the contractor's temporary way. Some years later he painted this vivid word picture of the problems we have already discussed and he recognised:

'A railway was to be built in my diocese, and suddenly four thousand new inhabitants were hutted in temporary villages in rural parishes. The Clergy of these parishes, already fully occupied, were unable to do anything. Besides, navvies are a peculiar class, somewhat like gypsies in their isolation and requiring special arrangements and special workers. I appointed a Chaplain, and I myself directed the Mission. The contractors built wooden churches at different points, and there I have preached to the most earnest and attentive congregations.'

The Bishop's plan

On returning to Uppingham, the Bishop began to put into operation plans to establish what he saw clearly as a great need: a Mission devoted entirely to the welfare of this multitude. A thorough investigation was begun, and with the aid of information supplied by the contractors a statement was prepared. This, together with the letter of appeal reproduced here, was circulated widely to raise funds.

As it transpired, the committee instituted to manage the Bishop's plan found it unnecessary to appoint the second minister. Certain lay-people had also taken an active interest, in particular someone Barrett mentioned as 'one

Palace, Peterborough,

JUNE 7TH, 1876.

DEAR SIR,

May I entreat your earnest and favourable consideration of the accompanying appeal.

The large and sudden influx of labourers employed upon the new lines of railway passing through many of our country parishes throws upon these, for some time to come, a burden for which their existing resources cannot be expected to provide.

On the other hand, the presence of a labouring population of nearly four thousand souls in our midst, calls for special effort on the part of the Church to provide them with the means of grace.

It is unfortunately but too certain that they will not, of their own accord, resort to our Parish Churches in search of these, and that they need, therefore, some missionary agency which may bring the message of the Gospel to their homes.

I am anxious, as suggested in the accompanying statement, which has been prepared at my request by a committee on the spot, to obtain for this purpose the services of at least two Missionary Clergymen and two Lay Readers, who should devote themselves to labouring amongst the " navvies " and their families along the new line of railway from Rushton to Manton.

I can only hope to obtain the necessary funds for this work by individual subscriptions, and I naturally make my first appeal to those who, either as owners of land along the line, or as shareholders in the railway, may feel that they have an interest in the spiritual welfare of the large multitude whom this enterprise is bringing amongst us.

I venture, therefore, earnestly to entreat your assistance in the effort now being made on their behalf.

I am,

Faithfully yours,

W. C. PETERBOROUGH.

The appeal letter of the Bishop of Peterborough.

who had authority on the works', and whose name I now believe to be Sir William Baker, of Barlow, Son & Baker, consulting engineers to various railways. He presented the matter to the contractors, who besides providing Mission chapels wherever they were needed, also subscribed a 'handsome annual sum' to the Bishop's Mission Fund. Lucas & Aird had shown themselves elsewhere to be among the few major contractors at the time to be responsive not only to the needs of their workforce, but also to be sympathetic towards the problems presented by the large numbers of strangers that they of necessity brought into the rural parishes. While they had a reputation as caring employers, it must be said that they had a vested interest in a sober and contented body of workers. Building railways was a dangerous business, best done by men in full charge of their faculties.

Between the autumn of 1875 and the summer of 1876 the mushrooming villages had become busy and lively communities. The main settlements were located at Wing Crossroads, Glaston Fox Covert, Glaston Field, Seaton, Gretton, Corby Wood, Oakley and Rushton, and along the entire course straggled shelters and primitive huts. Because of the primary importance of the building of Corby Tunnel, the settlement there was the first where the men gathered in large numbers. Here a chapel was erected, which also served the Gretton and Corby Mission. At first this Mission extended almost as far as Kettering, where a lay-reader – whose name I have yet to learn – ministered to the smallest and most remote settlement; this was Sir W. de Capell-Brooke's Mission. A second chapel was erected, and in due course the Midland Railway Company itself supplied a peripatetic reader who was active among the most scattered people, those who did not live near the main communities. However, Corby was the only place then where services were regularly held. Thus the works were served by '…three separate missionary agencies, occupying three distinct sections of the line, viz, "The Bishop's Mission", "The Corby and Gretton Mission", and "Sir W. de Capell-Brooke's Mission".' All of these agencies, collectively, became known as 'The Bishop of Peterborough's Railway Mission', according to the press coverage.

The Missioner arrives

As a result of subscriptions raised by his successful letter, the Bishop called from his curacy at Waltham-on-the-Wolds in Leicestershire the Reverend D. W. Barrett, he whose book it was that set me on my journey. Daniel William Barrett BA graduated from Trinity College, Dublin, in 1871, and attained his MA in 1875. From 1872 to 1873 he was curate of Bierley, Yorkshire, and afterwards of Waltham-on-the-Wolds, until called to the railway mission. His appointment was noted in the *Stamford Mercury* on 25 August 1876:

'KETTERING – THE REV D. W. BARRETT MA, late Curate of

Waltham, has been appointed by the Bishop of the diocese to the charge of the mission connected with the new railway works now in formation between Kettering and Manton.'

The original plan was that he should be based centrally in Gretton, and cover the whole line. However, it was decided that de Capell-Brooke's Mission beyond Corby should carry on its good work at that end, so Barrett took up residence in a vacant farmhouse at Glaston, known then as The Lodge, now Glaston Lodge. This house was to be his headquarters, being near to the railway settlement and conveniently central to the district in his care, and here he brought his bride on 9 August of the following year.

Meanwhile, the work on the line had made great progress. In August 1876, the same month that the Mission was established, the 65th half-yearly General Meeting of the Midland Railway Company was held at Derby. Mr Underwood, the engineer for lines under construction for the company, reported that: 'The works of the Kettering to Manton Railway were now in progress at all points. About one-fifth of the whole quantity of earth work had been executed and the bridges, arching and tunnels were proceeding satisfactorily.' As the works advanced, the Glaston section had become increasingly busy. More families arrived daily, and work on the approaches to the tunnel and the tunnel

itself gained momentum. By the time Barrett arrived, 'a large number of people had clustered thickly from Manton Station all along my new district.' There had been an immediate and generous response to the Bishop's appeal, and substantial monetary donations had been received from the public, together with bibles, books, and so on. At Glaston and Seaton the contractors had erected two more huts to be dedicated as chapels; these were, in fact, standard contractor's huts, at first indistinguishable from the others. They had also designated other huts in the settlements as reading rooms, school rooms, etc, and provided basic heating and lighting, as well as benches and tables.

Occasional evening services had been conducted at the Glaston chapel by the Rector, Rev Barnard Smith, before Barrett arrived, but they had met with little encouragement. The Rector was in failing health, and must have been quite overwhelmed by the sizeable and rapidly growing population of 'the strangers at his gate', which was another good reason to engage an additional, younger and more vigorous man to meet the exceptional circumstances. On 5 January 1877 the *Stamford Mercury* carried this report:

'UPPINGHAM: We regret to have to announce the death of a neighbouring clergyman, the Rev Barnard Smith,

Glaston Lodge Farm, where Barrett lived during his ministry. The large field in the foreground is one of the two hut sites at either end of Glaston Tunnel, and the picture was taken from the top of the spoil heap on the south side. *Author*

Rector of Glaston, to which he was presented in 1861, and Rural Dean of the Rutland 3rd Deanery. The deceased, who was 60 years of age, was the author of several well known school arithmetic books. The incumbency of Glaston, valued at £530 p.a. is in the gift of St Peter's College, Cambridge.'

The following week saw additional information regarding the late Rector. It seems that he was not only noted for his literary labours, but was

'...a staunch friend to educational pursuits, and also a most successful tutor to undergraduates reading for examinations in the University of Cambridge. Whilst Rector of Glaston, he was elected Chairman of the Board of Guardians of the Uppingham Union, and also of the Sanitary Committee, devoting his time, talents and experience for the benefit of rate-payers within the Union...'

Despite his condition, the Rector fully supported the work of the Mission, and acted as its secretary until his death.

During the interregnum at Glaston Rev Barrett took on the duties of the parish in addition to his own. While trawling through the Parish Registers, I felt quite moved to find Barrett's hand-writing when it appeared – my first tangible link with the man. His entries are in the registers from November 1876 until the following June, and after his signature appear the words 'Minister in Charge'.

Barrett's work begins

Barrett came to his new assignment with understandable trepidation. Although he felt that the bad reputation of the navvies was largely exaggerated, nevertheless it was not without foundation, and he was anxious about the initial encounters. He decided to make his first approaches as informal as possible. In this he was evidently successful: '...a friendly shake of the hand with one, a chat with another, a little while in this hut, a little while in that, soon brought us together.'

Glaston Church, were Rev Barrett took on the parish duties for a time following the death of Rev Barnard Smith. There are many railway graves in the churchyard, but only one has a memorial – see Chapter 12. *Author*

He walked up and down the works, and made great efforts to find common ground with the men. Realising that he would make no progress at all if he spoke to them from a superior position – for they were 'a fiercely independent race', and not at all the subservient class the agricultural labourers tended to be – he learned what he could from them about navvy life. He went into the tunnels, along the cuttings, and climbed the embankments. By showing himself eager to learn, and to meet the men literally on their own ground, he opened the way for teaching on his part; though he did not press religion on them. Steadily, a mutual confidence was built. Later he wrote in very glowing terms of the respect and attentiveness of the men, and in turn he clearly respected them. His book may appear patronising and sanctimonious to modern eyes, but this does not obscure what he obviously grew to feel, a deep and genuine regard for the navvies and their families.

The Missioner conducted the first service of his new ministry at Seaton, on 20 August 1876. Forty-two men, women and children attended, composed of parishioners, engineers, and foremen. But there were only two genuine navvies, and one of these was 'somewhat inebriated', and had to be escorted outside. This caused Barrett no little concern, and, as he reflected later, 'how could men in a similar unsatisfactory state of equilibrium' be prevented from interrupting future services? His anxiety proved unfounded, however, as the navvies themselves set up a rule that a drunken man should not enter a place of worship. The hymns at this service were 'sung with great feeling', and were accompanied by Barrett himself on a small harmonium purchased for the purpose at Uppingham on the previous Saturday. While he was disappointed that the service had not attracted more of the railway people, he expressed considerable encouragement that officials had been involved, for he saw this as a means of 'bringing in the right sort'. After this service, the Missioner and his party travelled the 2 miles back to the settlement at Glaston. Here they attempted to drum up a congregation for the evening. But 'we only mustered seven' – composed of children and the storekeeper and his wife, Mr and Mrs Hilling, who were to become the most stalwart supporters of the Mission, attending every service from first to last. They were among the very few who lived in the district for the whole time that the works were there.

Barrett could be forgiven for finding the experience of his first service at Glaston discouraging. 'The service at Seaton in the afternoon was enthusiastic compared to this,' he wrote. 'Seven people on two short benches in a corner of a building calculated to hold two hundred was not a particularly cheering sight.' Discouraged he might have been – deterred he was not! 'But the number was seven,' he continued positively, 'and it brought with it encouraging lessons, and its sacred symbolism was not forgotten.' There is a certain human

wistfulness when he compared the experience of these two services, 'and the missionary journey in between', with the large congregations and the 'grand old church' of his previous living. And a grand old church it is to this day, high in the Leicestershire Wolds, with its spire visible for miles around. He recognised a challenge, and rose to meet it, though he confessed to a struggle in his heart between courage and despair, for 'the surroundings might have appeared more natural had the scene been laid in the backwoods of Canada, or on a hillside of a lately acquired colony only just populated with English residents. In a home county of England it seemed hardly possible.' He was to draw the analogy of the similarity to a Canadian scene later. As he reflected upon the 'bright trappings and homely look' of the huts where the settlers lived, and compared them with the 'very bare walls and uninviting aspect of the chapels', he saw a need to make them not only more attractive, but also more appropriate for their purpose. These huts, identical to others provided by the management for all purposes, somehow had to persuade the prospective congregations to step over their thresholds. And so, during the next few weeks, the chapels were 'made bright with painted texts, hangings, and flowers'. But the days were growing shorter, and the nights were drawing in.

> 'As the autumn sun began to decline earlier, and the shades of night drew in more rapidly, we found it necessary to add to our fittings more means for lighting. Accordingly, a number of lamps were purchased, sufficient to throw a flood of cheerfulness over the room. I am a believer in the power of light. Every place of worship should be brightly lighted. To come from a cheerful, well lighted house, to a gloomy church at once depresses the spirits.'

He also saw the need for cleanliness – the chapels should be kept clean and fresh. In this he was supported by people coming forward to undertake the sweeping and general upkeep, no easy task in the middle of busy communities, built as they were in the open without paving or anything to prevent the mud of the surrounding area treading in. New people were coming into the works daily. As he walked around the 7 miles or so of his district, Barrett noticed how difficult it was to distinguish the chapels from other buildings. This, and a chance remark from a newcomer that Sunday seemed the same as any other day, prompted Barrett to make the chapels more prominent and by doing so emphasise the importance of Sunday. He therefore caused little wooden steeples or turrets to be erected over the basic huts, and in due course installed 'a single bell, chiming out its summons to prayer and praise'. The tallest possible scaffold poles were set beside the chapels, from which

'...every Sunday from dawn to dusk, winter and summer, were flown flags, with the device of a large red cross on a white background. These not only sent forth the message that it was Sunday, and attracted the attention of newcomers to the works, but also encouraged the Mission travellers as they made their way between the settlements ... and there was no point at which you could not see the sign floating above one or other of the Mission stations.'

Not content with all this, Barrett had the chapel at Glaston doubly whitewashed, and so it 'gleamed against its neighbours, which were black, being covered in tar'. This building

Seaton Chapel: Barrett had flags erected on the tallest scaffold poles to distinguish the chapels from the rest of the settlements.

became known, and was long remembered, as the Mission Cathedral. It pays to advertise...

For six months he worked single-handedly, then, as the *Grantham Journal* reported on 27 January 1877:

'The Bishop has appointed Mr John Bruster to assist the Missioner as Lay reader. Until recently Mr Bruster held a similar appointment at Dogsthorpe, under the Vicar of Peterborough. We understand that the Bishop has expressed his intention to visit the mission in person before long, and we doubt not that he will attract large congregations.'

He did indeed, as we shall see.

The Bishop had sanctioned a Short Form of Mission Service – hymns, prayers, readings, and an address. Barrett used this as a base for the early mission services. A choir was also secured, even though the congregations were continually changing. In a curious way this was an advantage, for the railway people had travelled extensively, and so had experience on which to draw. Welsh miners had come to bore the tunnels, and brought with them a strong tradition of singing in harmony. Navvies were noted for enjoying 'a bit of a sing', and there are many accounts of them whistling and singing at their work. Hymn practices were held after each service in preparation for the next, and many stayed on for this even if they were not members of the choir. The hymns of Moody and Sankey were particular favourites. In 1873 Dwight Lyman Moody and Ira David Sankey, American evangelists, had visited Great Britain on their first missionary tour, Moody preaching and Sankey singing, and had achieved great success.

It was almost guaranteed that there would be someone present who had a good musical ear and a strong voice, and one or two with the ability to play an instrument. Men came from Kent and the eastern counties, from Yorkshire and Lancashire, Cornwall and Devon – counties now well known for their brass and silver bands, an interest then in its infancy. So there was usually someone with a fiddle, or a penny whistle or a concertina, who could be prevailed upon to accompany the singing. Barrett had his harmonium, and later a piano was mentioned in one of the reports. But the wandering life soon called the men away to other works, so Barrett looked upon his ministry as one of reclamation and conversion rather than edification.

We now leap forward to 28 April 1877, when the *Grantham Journal* published a report on the first eight months of the Mission's activities. This had been distributed to the subscribers, and the *Journal* added its own comments:

'THE KETTERING TO MANTON RAILWAY – The Bishop of Peterborough's Mission: Though this mission only commenced on August 1st last, it seems desirable to place in the hands of the subscribers some account of the work that had been carried out up to December 31st 1876. The following agencies have been established: from August to the end of the year about seventy services were held at Seaton, Glaston, and Wing inclusive. Special services for the children have also been regularly conducted. A day school, supported by the contractors, is doing good work in Seaton huts. Funds are much needed for similar schools at Glaston, where there are a far larger number of children than can be accommodated in the village school. Sunday schools have been conducted in each of the Mission chapels, and from the number of children who attend appear to be appreciated. At the night schools, a good attendance of boys and young men, from 12 to 25 years of age, had always been secured. Two libraries, one at Glaston and one at Seaton, have been in working order for some months. It is desirable that a third should be established at Wing huts. During the winter six entertainments have been given, under the direction of the Missioner, consisting of readings, music, and recitations. Besides these there have been three magic lantern exhibitions. Two Christmas Trees and teas were given at Seaton and Glaston, to about 180 children from the works. By the kindness of a lady resident in the neighbourhood, a weekly mother's meeting and sewing class is held at Glaston huts. A lay-reader was appointed by the Bishop at the beginning of the present year to assist in the Mission, and has been mainly occupied at Seaton. In all these undertakings the Missioner has received a most willing personal and pecuniary help from private friends, and from the authorities and others connected with the works. The Bishop, who throughout has taken a lively interest in the Mission, has expressed a hope that he may be able in the course of the summer to visit the work in person. These facts are recorded with deep thankfulness, and it is hoped that the year 1877 will witness even more extended operations for the good of this interesting but too often much neglected class of our fellow countrymen. While thanking the subscribers for their already liberal aid, it is trusted they will be willing not only to continue that aid, but further to help the objects of the Mission by endeavouring to enlist the sympathy of others in so good a work. Subscriptions and donations will continue to be thankfully received by the Treasurers … to the account of "The Kettering and Manton Railway Missionary Fund". Parcels of bibles, books for the libraries, periodicals, and pictures suitable for the huts, will be received by the Rev D. W. Barrett, Glaston, Uppingham.'

Clearly the Mission was successfully carrying out its purpose, not only to meet the spiritual needs of the railway people, but also to bring social welfare, education and entertainment to the settlements. Of course, ever present, was the Victorian preoccupation with morals and inebriation. The powers that be found it always both advisable and necessary to counteract the wiles of the Demon Drink, and local bodies were very active in this regard. Thus we find that on Wednesday evening, 26 May 1875, a meeting in support of the Primitive Prohibitory Liquor Bill was held at the Lecture Hall, Uppingham, with Rev the Chancellor Wales presiding. Visiting clergy, notably Rev T. Hutton of Stilton, forcibly illustrated the evils of the liquor traffic from his own observations of many years. It was resolved that a petition be presented to Parliament in favour of the Bill. The Queen herself expressed interest in the Temperance movement:

'I am desired to thank you for placing in Her Majesty's hand works on a subject of the deepest importance to her and everyone in this country. It is impossible to the Queen not to be grateful to those who endeavour to mitigate the evil of such magnitude as the widely spread intemperance which unfortunately prevails...' (Article in the *Stamford Mercury*, 2 July 1875)

In the same issue appeared a report on a demonstration of the Uppingham Temperance Society, when they paraded through the town led by the Brigstock Brass Band, after which they 'repaired to the Middle Cricket Ground (kindly lent for the occasion by the Rev E. Thring)'. A public tea was given in a large marquee, to which upwards of 100 sat down.

This then was the climate into which the railway people came, these alien people, with their reputation for wildness and drunkenness, for whom Barrett had been required to set up his ministry. Again we must remind ourselves how transient were the people to whom the Mission was directed. As the needs of the works demanded, so men and their families assembled and dispersed. Sections of the line were started, progressed, and were completed. At the height of the activity it has been estimated that more than 4,000 men, women and children were distributed along the course.

The bride

The Missioner found time to get married, and brought his bride to The Lodge. He tells us himself that the railway people gave her a great welcome, but he gives no hint of who she was or how he met her. However, I found in the marriage column of the *Grantham Journal* for 4 August 1877 this announcement:

'Marriage: Barrett-Rendell. On 25th July, at St Andrews, Steyning (by the Rev A. M. Rendell, Rector of Coston, Leicestershire, brother of the bride, assisted by the Rev M. G. Vine, curate of Steyning, and the Rev B. Barrett, curate of Horncastle, brother of the bridegroom). The Rev D. W. Barrett, of Glaston, Uppingham, to Annie Sophia, daughter of Captain Rendell, RN.'

So she was the daughter of a naval captain; but how on earth, I wondered, did Barrett find time to meet, let alone court her? Steyning is a very long way from Rutland, but Coston is the neighbouring parish to Waltham-on-the-Wolds, from whence the bridegroom answered the Bishop's call to be his Missioner. Here was the probable answer. Even if there was no other connection, it is highly possible that Miss Rendell had met the curate of Waltham through her brother, some time between 1873 and 1876. A later and more detailed article revealed that the bride and groom had arrived in Glaston on 9 August, after a short honeymoon touring the Isle of Wight. A very hearty welcome awaited them at Glaston. The railway people had determined to make some expression of their kindly feeling, and presented the happy couple with 'a very handsome drawing-room clock, in ormolu and enamel, accompanied by an address'. The paper was 'glad to record this instance of true hearted and generous friendship from men who evidently appreciated the work of the Church in their midst'. Among other presents reported was a 'pretty electro-plated butter dish from the navvie children at Seaton'. I did not take particular notice of this gift, until I discovered some time later that the electro-plating process on a commercial scale had only commenced in Birmingham about 12 years before, so the children's gift was up-to-date as well as pretty. The young Mrs Barrett was immediately taken to the hearts of the railway families, and was soon deeply occupied with the activities expected of a Victorian clergyman's wife. We must remember that her husband was engaged in an exceptional ministry, so her parochial duties were of a special nature.

Untiring friends

Mr Barrett described as 'untiring friends' of the Mission the Hon W. C. Evans-Freke and Lady Victoria, his wife, of Bisbrooke Hall. He had been High Sheriff of Rutland, and after the railway was completed, the Mission over, and the workers long gone, he succeeded his brother, the 7th Baron Carbery of Castle Freke, County Cork and of Laxton Hall, Northamptonshire. As the 8th Baron, he was made a Deputy Lieutenant in County Cork, and a representative Peer for Ireland in the British Parliament. Lord Carbery died at Laxton Hall in 1894. All of that was to be in the future, but I find it an interesting insight into the calibre of a man who, as we will see, held a deep practical regard for the navvies and their families.

Lady Victoria held her title in her own right, for she was the daughter of the 3rd Marquis of Exeter. Typical of their era and station in life, they spared neither time nor money in support of the Mission and its activities. The works passed through their land, and while it was in progress the hundreds of railway people, for whom they held great social responsibility, were in a very true sense their neighbours. Mrs Barrett joined Lady Victoria in all the good works she had undertaken in the interests of the navvies' families, and it is recorded that she met with

Lady Victoria and the Hon William Evans-Freke. The Hon William became 7th Baron Carbery in 1889, while Lady Victoria held her title in her own right, being the daughter of the 3rd Marquis of Exeter. *Courtesy of Captain R. E. G. Boyles*

kindness from all quarters. Lady Victoria and other ladies worked tirelessly to bring comfort to the sick and the dying in the huts, and to help the navvy women and children. On the Northamptonshire side of the works, other ladies were also playing their part.

8
THE WORK CONTINUES

The Missioner had clearly consolidated the work entrusted to him. For a concise summary of what he achieved in the first 16 months of his ministry, we turn to the Chronicles of the Diocese of Peterborough, covering 15 December 1876 to 15 December 1877:

'THE KETTERING TO MANTON RAILWAY: THE BISHOP OF PETERBOROUGH'S MISSION. This Mission was started by the Bishop of the Diocese in August, 1876, to make adequate provision for the spiritual needs of the workmen and their families employed in making the new line of railway above mentioned. The following agencies have been appointed to effect this object:

i. SERVICES have been held at Glaston, Seaton, and Wing. At Wing, however, they have been very limited in number, owing to the want of a suitable room – a want which has recently been supplied by the Contractors. Services for children have been regularly conducted. The wooden chapels in which these services are held, are now licensed by the Bishop for the administration of Holy Communion, and Holy Baptism.

ii. DAY SCHOOLS supported by the Contractors, at Seaton Huts, and at Glaston Huts, from the Mission Fund and School Fees, are doing well.

iii. SUNDAY SCHOOLS have been conducted in each of the Chapels, and are thoroughly appreciated.

iv. NIGHT SCHOOLS, a fair average attendance of boys and young men has been secured. An Instruction Class for Girls is also held, which is well attended.

v. TWO LIBRARIES are carried on, one at Glaston and one at Seaton, with satisfactory results.

vi. One of the Church of England Temperance Society's Coffee Barrows has been started, and its success has already exceeded the anticipation of its supporters.

vii. ENTERTAINMENTS have been given under the direction of the Missioner, both for adults and children. A Reading Room is in active existence, at the chief centre of the works.

viii. A LAY READER was appointed by the Bishop at the beginning of 1877, and has been mainly and successfully occupied at Seaton.'

We know that all this was not accomplished single-handedly, but it really is remarkable what had been done under the circumstances that I have endeavoured to evoke.

Entertainments, pleasures and pastimes

Characteristically, Victorian entertainment – especially that which sprang from an official source – was likely to be of an 'uplifting and improving' nature, not only in the towns and cities, but here in this rural district. Uppingham, for example, had an active and enthusiastic Mutual Improvement Society, with its associated reading rooms, elocution

The interior of Seaton Mission Chapel.

classes, debating society, and interests in recitations, public readings and so on. Barrett wrote of pastimes at the huts on winter evenings, some of which we have looked at in an earlier chapter. Clearly the intention was to offer suitable leisure alternatives and entice the men away from drinking themselves into oblivion. Eventually a coffee barrow was introduced, and the men could partake of coffee and buns, and perhaps enjoy some music, for there was always someone who could play a fiddle or a concertina. Also, there were rehearsal gatherings for the more organised entertainment nights. Every other week the men worked night shifts, so rehearsals were not always easy to arrange. However, let us not be too beguiled by these idyllic scenes; the 'shants' were there, men did

get blind drunk, there were brawls, but now through the Mission an alternative was provided.

Looking at the organised entertainments, the general format of such an event was as follows. There was usually an opening piece on the pianoforte, often accompanied by another instrument. The programme was always well varied, with unaccompanied part songs, known as 'glee', quartets, solos, duets, a reading, and recitations, both 'grave and gay', as Barrett put it. He went to great pains to compare the navvy audience favourably with others. He said that the 'little 'uns' were encouraged to recite or sing a ditty. Once or twice there was a 'Negro entertainment' in one of the large workshops, given by the engineers, clerks, and others on the staff. In

Right This corrugated iron hut once stood on the Seaton Road, Glaston, and is said to have been the Mission reading room. *Author*

Below right Inside was the remains of a fireplace. Clearly these are not Victorian bricks, so the hut must have been in use in comparatively recent times. *Author*

addition to these home-made entertainments, there were regular lectures, penny readings, and magic lantern shows, usually given by the Missioner himself, and duly reported in the press.

Thus almost every week something was going on, in the shape of 'wholesome entertainment', at one or other centre of the works, and never without a numerous audience. When you come to read the chapter devoted to the weather, you may well find this remarkable, as I did. The hut-dwellers came in crowds to the entertainments, as did people from the surrounding villages. The press reported some of these events, as here in the *Grantham Journal* of 10 February 1877:

'THE KETTERING AND MANTON RAILWAY MISSION: an entertainment consisting of readings, recitations and songs was given at the Glaston Mission Room, on Tuesday, 30th ult, in the presence of a large and orderly gathering of railway people. The programme was a good one, and was carried out to the satisfaction of all present – a similar entertainment, in connection with the Bishop of Peterborough's Mission, was given at Seaton on Wednesday 7th, inst, when the room was very full, and a thoroughly enjoyable evening was spent...'

The village people were encouraged to contribute music and recitations. Thus we

find excellent examples of interaction between the railway people and the local communities, a clear indication of how the influence of the Mission had overcome much of the suspicion and prejudice referred to in earlier chapters. Indeed, sometimes, as here, the locals put on the whole show themselves:

'On one occasion the entire entertainment was undertaken by members of the Mutual Improvement Society in a neighbouring town (Uppingham). When once the better qualities and the higher tastes of the navvies became known, as well as the lower and less pleasing, the people around got to regard them in their true light, and united in trying to make their temporary residence a happy and improving one.'

It is difficult to comprehend the great numbers of children living in the huts and sharing the hard life of the works, and it is good to learn that there were special occasions of great delight provided for them during their brief stay in the neighbourhood. Navvy children, as others of the labouring classes, were expected to grow up all too soon and take on arduous work. For the children of the huts there were some occasions of pure delight, and the local papers reported on some of them, as here in the *Grantham Journal* of 27 January 1877:

'THE KETTERING AND MANTON RAILWAY MISSION – On Tuesday, Jan 16th, the children living in the huts at Glaston and Wing were invited to tea in the Glaston Mission Room. There were a hundred children present. After tea the prizes, gained by the scholars at the Sunday and Night Schools were distributed by Lady Victoria Evans-Freke. After this, a large Christmas Tree, beautifully illuminated, and heavily laden with presents, was provided, and caused great delight to all... On Thursday 25th a similar entertainment was given to the children at Seaton, when about seventy sat down to tea, and passed a very happy evening. These gatherings are managed by the clergyman in charge of the Mission, and their success is greatly enhanced by the efficient and willing help which is always readily afforded to him by the members of his congregation and the authorities on the works... A lecture on astronomy was given by the Rev D. W. Barrett on Wednesday 17th to an attentive audience. The lecture was illustrated by some excellent magic lantern slides,

which appeared to be appreciated by those present.'

It was therefore not all toil and arduous labour, and not all the social activities were provided by the Mission. On Monday 19 November 1877 one such event took place, and I present it in its entirety as an example not only of a pleasant social occasion, but how formal were the structures of companionable events in those days. The *Grantham Journal* again provides a graphic description:

'GLASTON: SOCIAL EVENING – A number of the sub-contractors and foremen connected with the railway tunnel here, under the course of construction, met at "The Three Horseshoes" (Mrs Warren's), to enjoy a social hour or two. The repast was of excellent description, and consisted of six courses. After the cloth was removed, a "toddy" and pipes were introduced, and good fellowship was the order of the evening. Mr D. Jewett was voted in the chair, and was ably assisted by Mr W. Stafford, of Glaston, as vice-chairman. The company numbered 32. Several others would have been present, but were obliged to send letters of apology on account of pressing business. After the usual loyal and patriotic toasts had been given from the chair, and responded to in the English fashion, Mr Hilling was called upon for a song, and rendered "The Husband and Wife" in his best style, and received an enthusiastic encore; Mr Hilling substituted "Little Nell". Mr Frank Howe caused much amusement with "I Think I Have seen You Before", Mr Button gave "Tom Bowling". Mr Turner well sustained his reputation when he sang "I Have Been Sleeping". Mr Point followed with "I Have Been Walking", a parody on the previous song. Mr Herbert was warmly applauded in "The Butcher and the Baker". Mr Dunne was cheered in his "Out of Sorts", as also was Mr Stone, with "The Smuggler's Boy", Mr Jones, "Work to be Contented" and Mr Douglas, "The Broken-hearted

Keelman". Mr Easter, Inspector, then addressed the company on the subject of "Unity". He remarked he was not going to advance a single word on union societies, but wished simply but earnestly to impress upon the company the great value of hearty co-operation amongst workmen on the work itself. Mr Stafford spoke to a like effect, and the sentiments of both speakers were fully endorsed by the party of railway veterans, for no man understands this and carries it out to its truest spirit better than they. The company then joined in singing "Auld Lang Syne", and "The Queen". Votes of thanks were tendered to the Chairman, and the meeting separated at 9 o'clock, after fixing an early date for a reunion.'

Do we see in the remarks of Mr Easter and Mr Stafford a hint that there may be dissatisfaction among the workforce? Were trades unions raising their heads? If so, this is the only intimation I have found of it.

The winter of 1877-78 was a long and bitter one, but organised social events and entertainments nevertheless took place. Another example of local people providing the entertainment at the huts was when Uppingham Elocution Class, with some musical friends, presented a long and varied programme at Glaston, before an audience of about 200 engineers, work people, their families and villagers. The applause, the press tells us, was hearty! Among the items was the trial scene from *The Merchant of Venice*, and 'interest was sustained throughout'. One wonders how it would have been received in our day by a similarly composed audience…

The Christmas and New Year festivities for the children took place as on the previous year. This time 140 children at Glaston and 80 at Seaton enjoyed 'an excellent tea and splendid Christmas Tree, beautifully illuminated and laden with presents for young and old, both children and their parents being invited.' There was not a repeat of these events the following winter. The children had nearly all gone, dispersed with their families among other works far away, and only a very few railway people remained.

Distinguished visitors

Every Lent, as it came round, a series of sermons was preached by visiting clergy, who had expressed interest in the Mission, and had been particularly invited. Some of them travelled considerable distances to speak in the chapels, but these special services were not always reported in the press. Barrett himself tells us that during the course of the Railway Mission, 25 different clergy, including Bishops, Priests and Deacons, addressed the congregations during its progress. At least two of these were of national significance.

The late Rector of Glaston, Rev Barnard Smith, was succeeded in June 1877 by Rev Christopher Wordsworth. He, it so happened, was the son of the Bishop of Lincoln, also Christopher Wordsworth, a most distinguished cleric and scholar of his day, and nephew of the poet William. His influence is still with us today in the form of well-known hymns. Naturally, the Bishop came to Glaston to visit his son; he was taken on a brief tour of the adjacent part of the works, which was developing rapidly, and showed great interest both in the work of the navvies and that of the Mission. He accepted an invitation to

The Right Reverend Christopher Wordsworth, Bishop of Lincoln, one of many distinguished clergy who preached in the wooden chapels and took interest in the Mission. *Author's collection*

conduct evensong at the 'Mission Cathedral', so on Sunday 12 September 1877 there he was, this nationally famous man, on a Rutland hillside in a simple wooden chapel addressing simple British workmen.

Barrett's words describe the occasion most vividly:

'The service, which was held in the evening, was very bright and hearty, and there was a large congregation of the work-people and their families, besides some few from the neighbouring village. The Bishop adapted himself to his audience in a wonderful manner, and gave a very touching and eloquent address from Isaiah xl 1-8, laying special stress on the words: "The voice of him that crieth in the wilderness, Prepare ye the way of the Lord, make straight in the desert a highway for our God. Every valley shall be exalted, and every mountain and hill shall be made low, and the crooked shall be made straight, and the rough places plain; and the glory of the Lord shall be revealed, and all flesh shall see it together." He spoke to the men in stirring language, using abundant and graphic illustrations from the varied character of the works, telling them plainly but lovingly some of their "rough places" and "crooked ways". Once he spoke in most touching simplicity for some few minutes to the young... The earnest tones and venerable form of the Bishop, as he stood habited in a large old-fashioned surplice ... seemed somehow to carry one back in thought to the early days of the Christian Church...'

'Make straight in the desert a highway ... every mountain and hill shall be made low ... the crooked shall be made straight, and the rough places plain' – biblical words that describe perfectly the work that was being done by the workmen who listened to him so attentively. The following day, the Bishop and his family, with Rev and Mrs Barrett, others on the Mission staff and several of the senior engineers, made an excursion along the temporary line in an open truck drawn by an engine. He spoke to the men individually, shook many hands, and showed a great interest in all he saw. The Bishop was then 70 years old, and created a great impression with all he met.

The navvies' Bishop

A few weeks later the Right Reverend William Connor Magee, Bishop of Peterborough, the 'Navvies' Bishop' himself, made his long anticipated visitation. He had drawn up a very full programme for himself, as he intended to preach at all the chapels of the Mission. He stayed at Bisbrooke Hall with Lady Victoria and her husband, the Hon William Evans-Freke. Here was one of the most celebrated orators of the day, both in the pulpit and the House of Lords, famous throughout the kingdom. It was therefore a wonderful thing for such a national figure to preach in the humble wooden chapels. Word had gone up and down the line, and crowds

The 'Navvies' Bishop' himself, the Right Reverend William Connor Magee. *Peterborough Museum and Art Gallery*

came from all around the district to see and hear him. This was not only an important occasion for the Mission, but significant stages of the works were also being reached.

Although there is some repetition of what we already know, I reproduce in full this long article from the *Grantham Journal* of 27 October 1877, for it is not only an eye-witness account of the Bishop's visit, but also a fine review of the story so far:

'It may be known to most of our readers that a large number of men are employed in the county of Rutland in making new lines of railway. The most important works are going on between Kettering and Manton, owing to the extension of the Midland system. In order to accommodate the people employed in this extensive undertaking, on which are two tunnels over a mile in length, and others of several hundred yards, besides a splendid viaduct nearly three quarters of a mile long, and numerous large bridges and steep embankments, wooden villages have been erected at various centres along the line. For the most part these hut villages are at a distance from the Parish Churches, and consequently are more or less out of reach of the parochial system of the Church. In the summer of last year, when the Bishop of Peterborough was at Uppingham, he saw the pressing necessity there was of a more adequate provision for the spiritual needs of the railway work-people employed in the neighbourhood. He accordingly set to work to raise funds for the purpose, and was soon enabled to appoint a clergyman to the work. For more than a year a mission has been carried on by the Rev D. W. Barrett, and others, under the Bishop's direction, and on Sunday, October 21st, his Lordship visited the scene of the Mission in person. Mission Chapels have been erected by the contractors at Glaston, Seaton, Wing, and other centres along the line. The Bishop preached in each of the chapels named to crowded congregations of the workmen and their families. The services

were very bright and hearty, and the simple eloquence and earnestness of the Bishop secured the profound attention of all who heard him. During the morning service at Wing, he appointed a layreader [sic] to work at Corby, a mission station near Kettering where highly successful work has been carried on under the direction of the Rev B. E. W. Bennett, the Rector of the parish. At this service the Bishop spoke of the various ways in which the laity could and ought to aid the clergy in their responsible office. On the divine, authoritative and distinctive character of the office and work of the clergy, he showed that for any true and lasting success, the clergy and laity must work together in one common cause – for one common Master. In the afternoon, at Seaton, he preached on the parable of the Sower, and applied the subject to the circumstances and objects of the Mission in a most striking manner. Both at Wing and at Seaton the Bishop and clergy robed in one of the huts, and formed a procession to the chapel, many of the workmen following them in. In the evening the Bishop addressed the congregation at Glaston, where the chapel was filled to excess, several people being unable to get in. As this is the centre of the Mission, and is commonly spoken of by the men as the "Cathedral", and is the most populous station, he preached with special reference to the character of the Mission, taking as his text Revelations I: verses 17 and 18. After speaking of the missionary career of St John the Evangelist, he applied words of encouragement "Fear not" to the mission when he set it amongst those to whom he was speaking. He showed further, how these same words, from that same Voice, would also comfort and support those who were doing any work for God, in what ever capacity they were engaged on in the mission, and he exhorted one and all to the knowledge of Jesus Christ as the First and Last in all that they undertook, whether in Church work or in the silent and more hidden work of the individual soul. It need hardly be recorded that he was listened to throughout with the most rapt attention. At all the services large numbers of men were present, and the Bishop spoke of it as a gratifying fact; his words especially addressed to the young men anxious to do what was right, to bear witness for Christ, and yet be surrounded and pressed sore by the temptations incident to the life of those living in large numbers in huts, and engaged on public works, will not easily be forgotten. The well known hymns selected for use at the services were joined in most fervently by all present.

On the following day, the Bishop, accompanied by Mrs Magee, the mission staff, and some of the chief authorities on the works, made an excursion on the temporary line towards Manton, in open trucks drawn by an engine. The party consisted of Bishop and Mrs Magee, Lady Victoria and the Hon W. C. Evans-Freke, R. Stannard, Esq, C. J. Wills, Esq, C. H. Meares, Esq, the Rev and Mrs Barrett, and the Rev Leonard Addison. The various branches of the works were inspected, and the novel sight was witnessed of a bishop going into the tunnel to see the navvie at his work in the bowels of the earth. He was most heartily welcomed all along the works, and many a rough hand grasped his with the feeling that he was their friend who had their best interests at heart. On the evening of the same day he received a deputation from the men, bearing an address from the representative members of the congregations, thanking him for the active interest in their welfare. Messrs S. Hilling, J. Stone, H. Plowman, and H. Finch were chosen as the deputation. On Tuesday he left Bisbrooke Hall, where he had been a guest...'

This article was one of the first to record facts about the works, as well as to review the progress of the Mission. By the mid-1870s, as I suggested earlier, the Victorian readers were probably as blasé about railway building as we in the early 21st century have become about the space programme. You will recall that very little was remarked upon when the work began, despite the national and economic importance of the new line, and the great obstacles that had to be overcome in its construction. However, for some time there had been determined moves afoot to take the Word of the Lord to the displaced labouring classes. Many thousands had left the land and their roots to seek employment in the growing cities, and Missionaries were therefore sent to darkest England as well as to darkest Africa; the Mission directed towards the railway workers was a progression of this movement. Yet I suspect, perhaps cynically, that until two significant Establishment figures showed personal involvement, and thus imbued the men and the work with a certain amount of respectability, the press, on the whole, was content merely to mention passing incidents of crime or accidents.

To return to the article, and pick up on some of the points it highlights – there is a hint of the poor conditions and moral risk associated with living in crowded huts. I am sure that this refers particularly to the 'shants', which I looked at in more detail in the section on hut life. The chapel at Wing, a want of which was noted in the Diocesan chronicle, was now operational, and I will take it into account later in this chapter. Barrett tells us that the lay-reader appointed at Wing was Mr W. Chapman, who was to work among the men at Corby. Corby's Rector, Rev B. E. W. Bennett, is here named as director of 'the mission station near Kettering', whereas previously the Gretton and Corby Mission, under the leadership of Rev Arthur White, had extended almost to Kettering. So it had become a separate entity, an indication of how dense the railway population had become in that part of the works. The Rev Leonard Addison had succeeded Rev Arthur White as the incumbent at Gretton in 1876. It was estimated that more than a thousand men were employed on Corby Tunnel and the cuttings on either side. It is possible that the duties were shared there as the works reached their height, but as yet I have no evidence of this.

Lady Victoria Evans-Freke presented gifts and prizes to navvy children. She, Mrs Barrett and other ladies worked together to organise sewing groups and so on for the navvy women. *Courtesy of Captain R. E. G. Boyles*

The excursion party is interesting, and we have met some of them before. The Evans-Frekes of Bisbrooke Hall, which is nearer to Glaston than to Bisbrooke, had been from the outset staunch benefactors to, and supporters of, the Mission, and firm friends to the railway people. It was Lady Victoria who was the unnamed 'kindly lady, resident in the neighbourhood', who had set up the weekly mother's meetings and sewing classes at the Glaston Huts, and donated gifts, treats and prizes to the children. She helped with the schools, organised local ladies and hut women into working parties for the benefit of the railway families, and did many acts of charity towards the sick and injured of the Glaston and Wing settlements. The Hon William, her husband, was himself extremely active in his support of the charitable work of the Mission, and was one of the principal landowners through whose estates this part of the line

passed. He was a magistrate, and held much influence. Mr Stannard had become Mr Eagle's successor in 1877, as local agent to Lucas & Aird, and as such he was superintendent to the whole line. Mr Wills came under him, and was agent for the Corby section. Rev Leonard Addison had become the incumbent at Gretton in 1876, succeeding Rev Arthur White. Mr Meares was one of the senior engineers. Of the deputation, we have met Mr Hilling before: he was the company storekeeper at Glaston Huts, and with his wife was deeply involved with the Mission. They took on the caring of the Chapel, never missed a service in all the three years they were there, and were firm and practical friends to the hut dwellers. Mr Stone, Mr Plowman and Mr Finch were foremen at Glaston at the time. Mr Stone later died in the fall down the shaft.

Although Barrett's official ministry ended at the edge of Gretton parish, much of the line lay beyond, though still covered by the Bishop of Peterborough's Railway Mission. Great numbers of men worked on the Gretton and Corby section, most of them living in the largest settlement on the line at Corby Wood – Barrett's 'Canadian forest scene', a description that was probably not exaggerated, as this area was all part of the medieval forest of Rockingham, fragments of which, despite the ravages of iron-ore extraction, the steel industry, and the development of Corby new town, remain to this day. Here the Mission was conducted, as we know, by the Rector of Corby, Rev B. E. W. Bennett, assisted by Mr W. Chapman, the 'hard working Lay-reader'. In the early summer of 1878 it was announced that the 'Navvy Bishop' himself was to visit this part of the works, and would hold a special service for the men.

It was to take place on Wednesday 5 June at 5 o'clock, so that as many of the men could attend as possible. From different parts of the line they came, in truck loads, all in their working clothes. Barrett tells us that they jumped out of the wagons and ran across the field where the settlement was, to get a good place in the chapel. There were about 300 present, including the press, who reported the occasion. Such a crowd was there that one of the end walls had to be taken down so that those who had to remain outside could hear the Bishop's words. The service opened with a hymn, and suitable prayers were said by Rev Bennett. The Bishop followed with his address, speaking with 'great earnestness and vivid force', showing how much he and the navvies had in common. There followed another hymn. The service lasted about three-quarters of an hour, and was concluded by the benediction, after which the men dispersed, some to their work, and some to their homes, 'doubtless much encouraged by their chief pastor'.

Three days later, on Friday 7 June, a most historic event took place; historic not only for the Mission in particular, but for public works in general. The Rites of Confirmation were administered by the Bishop at Glaston Mission Chapel to 26 candidates from the works and 13 from the village. It is believed that this was the first event of its kind ever to take place on a railway works. Both the service at Corby Wood and at the Glaston ' Mission Cathedral' were attended by clergy from all round the district.

The chapel at Wing

When Barrett took up his ministry in 1876 the contractors had already provided chapels at Glaston, Seaton, Corby Wood, and one other on the Northamptonshire side, the location of which I am not sure. For some months the colony at Wing was not considered large enough to require its own, and those who wished to do so walked the couple of miles or so to join the worship at Glaston. However, in 1877 the work on the cutting towards Wing Tunnel and the tunnel itself commenced, so the population increased rapidly, and soon there was a large and growing community. But there was no chapel. By the end of his first year Barrett was holding services where he could, 'now in the common living room of one of the huts, sometimes in the pay office, often on the slopes of the railway bank, and for several Sundays in the summer we pitched a tent, kindly supplied by the contractors, and held service in that.' Singing and speaking under canvas was difficult, but the shelter ensured a congregation in all weathers, he wrote.

In the autumn of 1877 the contractors ordered that a chapel should be erected at the Wing settlement, and a redundant hut was duly sent from Corby Wood. As it was being drawn up the hill towards Wing the wagon that bore it broke down before the hilltop was reached, causing much concern. However, eventually it was erected on site. After considerable renovation, it was dedicated as a house of prayer, and Barrett tells us that 'soon it was standing with its little turret and open porch under the shelter of the hill at Wing crossroads'. The first service was held on the last Sunday in September 1877, which was a combined thanksgiving both for the chapel and the harvest. From that day until the end of 1878 regular worship was held there.

Thanksgivings and presentations

Harvest festivals and their associated rejoicing are now such an established part of the church calendar that it seems they have always been so. There is scarcely a church in which a harvest thanksgiving is not held in one form or another, and the harvest hymns are as familiar as Christmas carols. But it was not always so. In 1843 the vicar of Morwenstow in Cornwall, Rev Robert Stephen Hawker, was possibly the first to introduce this festival. Twenty-four years later, harvest celebrations took place on the Kettering to Manton line in each of the wooden chapels on the works.

On 12 October 1878 the press reported:

'Harvest Thanksgiving – The first Harvest Thanksgiving Service on the Mission this year for the blessings of the harvest was observed at Seaton Mission Chapel on Wednesday evening last. Unfortunately the weather was very rainy, and most of the men had got wet in the afternoon, which prevented many of them coming, still the chapel was full. The service was very bright, and the decorations were very tastefully arranged, under the direction of Mr J. Bruster, lay-reader. The service was read by the Rev D. W. Barrett and Mr Bruster, and the sermon was preached by the Rev W. M. Croome, vicar of Syston,

The Chapel at Wing, where Bishop Magee preached morning service during his tour of October 1877. Note its flag and little bell turret.

Wing crossroads was one of the hut sites. The tunnel runs beneath the field beyond the hedge on the right. Wing is behind us, Preston to the left, and Manton ahead. *Author*

whose earnestness and appropriate address riveted the attention of the congregation throughout. The Offertory was for the "Abercarne Colliery Accident Fund". We understand that a similar service will be held at Glaston Chapel tomorrow, when the preacher will be the Rev and Worshipful the Chancellor Wales. The Offertory is to be devoted to the same object.'

Today, the offertory is also an integral part of a service that we recognise and take for granted. However, it was the same vicar of

Morwenstow who was almost the first incumbent in England to establish it as such in the early 1840s. Thus, remote as it was, the Mission was quite up to date in its worship.

By now, certain sections of the works were coming to a close, and the railway people began to disperse. The same issue of the *Grantham Journal* that covered the harvest celebration also reported:

'KETTERING AND MANTON RAILWAY MISSION: Presentation – A very interesting event took place in the reading room, in connection with the

Glaston Mission Chapel, on 27th September. A number of the members of the congregation met together to make a presentation to Mr and Mrs Hilling, in recognition of their unceasing attention to the wants of those who meet together to worship in the Chapel. Mr Hilling has acted as one of the Chapel wardens, librarian, Sunday school teacher, and in various other ways has been a true friend to the Church. To his wife, the neat and cleanly appearance of the Chapel and its fittings is mainly due. The proposal to present them with a family Bible and an electroplated teapot was warmly taken up, and subscriptions flowed in at once from many railway people and others to provide for the cost of the articles, which were both very elegant. The presents were acknowledged with much emotion, and Mr Hilling returned heartfelt thanks for himself and his wife for the kindness which had been shown them, and said what little they had done was from a sense of duty. We hope they will both live long, and be as useful as they have been at Glaston.'

Then, on 19 October 1878 we read:

'KETTERING AND MANTON RAILWAY – Glaston Mission Chapel – a crowded congregation met at the chapel on Sunday evening, to thank Almighty God for the blessings of the Harvest. The majority of the hut population of the district were present, as well as friends from the village. The Chapel was bright with tasteful decorations, and the service was of the usual hearty and congregational type. The preacher was the Chancellor of the Diocese, the Rev the Worshipful W. Wales, Rector of Uppingham, who delivered a very telling sermon on the lessons of the harvest-tide, and referred in touching language to the recent sad catastrophes by land and sea. The Offertory was devoted to the "Abercarne Colliery Accident Fund", and realised the handsome sum of £5 2s 5d.'

Closing celebrations

Between June 1877 and June 1878, the work was at its height, then, from the 4,000 people it has been suggested were employed for a few weeks, the works steadily began drawing to a close, as major constructions reached completion. Many of the people present at the services would soon be scattered, gone to other works, perhaps in other lands. As they finished their sections, whole gangs of 80 or 90 navvies packed up their belongings and their families, and moved on. Barrett wrote poignantly of how a 'hive of industry' one week became quiet and empty the next, with only rubbish blowing in the wind and a stark new structure to show where it had been. In most cases the men just went away. In others, however, particularly when the work had entailed grave danger or more than usual difficulty, a ceremony of some kind was deemed appropriate before they dispersed. The latter months of 1878 saw several such events. At least one, associated with the great viaduct, was of a secular nature, and we looked at that in Chapter 6. Others took the form of a special Mission service, and these we look at here.

On 28 July 1878 a particular milestone was safely reached. Wing Tunnel, though shorter than the others, had been the most difficult to construct. The work was the heaviest and the pressures the greatest of all the other constructions on the line, and it is quite remarkable that the tunnel was completed without serious accident. A special thanksgiving service was arranged to take place actually inside the tunnel. The press was in attendance, for by now both the line and the Mission had at last caught the public attention.

'...there was a large number of people present, many coming in their working dress. The service consisted of a short Mission form, supplemented by some popular hymns, the singing of which was most striking. The harmonium was played by one of the miners engaged on the railway. A sermon was preached by the Rev D. W. Barrett, on the words

"What mean ye by this service?" (Exodus xii.26). After giving briefly a few precedents from Holy Scripture for services of a special character, and referring to the probability of even subterranean services, instancing the probable worship of the prophets hid by fifty in a cave, the witness of the "dens and caves" in which holy men of old sought refuge, the history of the Catacombs – he went on to say, in some respects there were parallels and contrasts between the case of the Israelites in Egypt and that of the workmen engaged in the construction of that tunnel, eg their occupation on public works, their different treatment, their deliverance from death, their exodus, their wandering in search of a new home, their duty of bearing witness in their wandering for the name and Church of their God. He then showed how the service was intended to be one of commemoration, of thanksgiving and instruction. The congregation was most orderly and attentive.'

The fact that this tunnel had been bored through and bricked without either loss of life or serious injury was indeed cause for both thanksgiving and rejoicing; the difficulties encountered in its construction are related in another chapter. By the early autumn, another superb feat of civil engineering was nearing completion, and plans were made to commemorate this in a striking though appropriate manner. Glaston Tunnel, at 1,846 yards, is the second longest on the entire route, and represented a huge section of the works. Though 79 yards shorter than Corby Tunnel, the mining was of an exceedingly dangerous nature, involving specialised and difficult techniques. Sadly, its construction had claimed lives, and was beset by other serious accidents. It is remarkable not that accidents occurred, but that they were comparatively few. Once again the *Grantham Journal* sent forth an intrepid reporter, who recorded one of the most notable events, not only in the history of the Mission, but in the building of the line. The occasion was so striking, and the account so graphic, that the article is here reproduced in full:

'STRIKING SERVICE AT GLASTON TUNNEL – From time to time we have given our readers short sketches of the work of the Church amongst the railway men employed on the Kettering and Manton line in progress of construction through the county of Rutland. The work at the Manton end is now approaching completion. Last week, one of the tunnels over a mile in length – which passes one hundred and fifty feet beneath the parish of Glaston – was successfully bored through, and all the mining operations completed. It was thought desirable that the event should be celebrated by a special service, before the workmen who had been engaged in it had left the scene of their labours for other railways. Accordingly, a short notice was issued, announcing that a special Mission service would be held in the tunnel on Sunday evening, September 8th, at half-past five, and that it was intended to be, as in the case of a similar gathering in Wing tunnel a few weeks before, a service of commemoration, thanksgiving and instruction; and an earnest hope was expressed that the men would attend in large numbers. The invitation was accepted, and the whole hut population of Glaston and the neighbouring huts made the descent into the open ends of the tunnel, as well as nearly all the railway people living in the villages round, and large numbers besides flocked in from all quarters. Every class was well represented, from the engineers and agents down to the humblest navvy, miner, and bricklayer who had taken part in the work. It was computed by many who were there, and who were competent to judge, that there were no less than a thousand people present. Unfortunately, several heavy peels of thunder were heard towards evening, and the sky looked very black and threatening, and a great number of people turned back, fearing a storm was gathering, or there would have been many more. Happily the rain did not fall, and they who continued their journey reached the tunnel in safety, and were enabled to take part in this remarkable service. After penetrating some distance into the gloom, over the rough burnt ballast, the congregation approached the space in the tunnel where the service was to be held. This was lighted up with lamps hanging from the walls, and candles were also stuck upon them in the usual miner's candlestick of clay. The pulpit was a log of timber placed on a few bricks and the prayer desk an upturned wheel-barrow. A number of seats were arranged along the sides with a passage up the middle, but owing to their insufficiency, hundreds could not find room and were obliged to stand. The service commenced with the hymn "How sweet the name of Jesus sounds!" This was followed by the order for a Mission service appointed by the Bishop for use in the diocese, containing psalms appropriate for the occasion. The selected lesson was Isaiah xl verses 1-18, and was read by the Rev and Worshipful W. Wales, the Chancellor of the diocese, and Rector of Uppingham. The latter part of the service, from the Apostles' Creed, was said by the Rev J. B. D. Stansfeld. The clergy were habited in their surplices, which had a weird and striking effect in contrast with the deepening darkness of the long recess behind them. After the lesson, Bonar's grand hymn, "A few more years shall roll", was sung with heart-touching solemnity, as they who sang it were standing between two spots where, a few months ago, two poor fellows falling headlong down the shafts were suddenly summoned to eternity. The hymn before the sermon was "Art thou weary?" The preacher was the Rev D. W. Barrett, curate-in-charge of the Mission, who took for his text, "He brought me also out of the horrible pit, out of the mire and clay; and set my feet upon the rock and

ordered my goings. And he hath put a new song into my mouth. Even a thanksgiving unto our God. Many shall see it and fear: and shall put their trust in the Lord" (Psalm xl 2,3,4), and was listened to throughout with earnest attention. After a few introductory remarks, he first applied the words to the occasion of the gathering of the day, speaking of the great danger, the merciful deliverance, the joyful song, and the new life which should be the result. At this point in the address, he called on the people to make the walls of the very place where so many great dangers had been undergone and deliverances effected, re-echo a better and a holier song than they had often done in weeks gone by; while they stood now, and lifted up their voices in heartfelt thanks to God in the words of the "Old Hundredth Psalm". The appeal was responded to in a way which none who were there can easily forget. When the hymn was ended, the preacher proceeded to make the more spiritual application of the text, taking the same chief thoughts to direct him in pressing home the danger of a life of sin, the need for deliverance from it, and the happier and holier life to which Jesus the Deliverer would lead, if only His guidance were accepted, and the journey commenced on the "narrow way" leading to the eternal home. At the conclusion of the sermon, the Mission hymn, "I was a wandering sheep", ended the musical portion of the service, the harmonium being played by Mrs Kingston. A few appropriate collects were said, and two special prayers were offered up, the first on behalf of the those who had been engaged on the works, and who were soon to be scattered far and wide in the world, the second for the safety of those who in future years should be called to "pass by that way" in their travels in pursuit of their lawful undertakings. The Rev the Chancellor then pronounced the benediction, and so a very solemn yet joyful service terminated.'

'Exodus'

The line by now was nearing completion. There was still much to do by way of finishing off, but the heavy work was over. From about June 1878 the work wound down, and, as their sections closed, the railway people left in their hundreds, just as they had arrived. All along the works huts fell into ruin and machinery was sent off to other sites. The Mission itself came to an end.

From the *Grantham Journal* of 28 December 1878:

'Lyddington – we understand that the Rev D. W. Barrett, who has been conducting the Bishop of Peterborough's railway mission, has been licensed to the above parish. We trust his ministrations will prove acceptable to the people and that the Church work in the place will prosper…'

April 28, 1879.

THE RIGHT REV. LORD BISHOP OF PETERBOROUGH.

Will you kindley except this Bible as a token of respect from a few of the old Hands left on the Kettering and Manton Railway as we feel we should like to make some acknoglement for the great Intrest you have taken in our Spiritual Wellfare.

We think as Railway Men it tis a great Honour for a Bishop to Come Amoung us all Much More to take the Intrest you have done we all Sinceley thank you for having a Mission Amoungest us which we hope will be a blessing to Many of us and we Sincerley hope you will **not** reget for what you have done

Signed on behalf of the Congegrations work man

S. H——.

H P——.

When the men began to disperse to other sites, they made a presentation to 'their' Bishop, accompanied by this very touching letter. Do note the spelling. 'S.H—' was Mr Hilling, keeper of the 'shant' at Glaston; he and his wife took great pride in the chapel. 'H.P—' was Mr Henry Plowman, one of the foremen on Glaston Tunnel.

9
THE WEATHER

We know by now how many railway people there were on these works, that thousands of men, and hundreds of women and children came here. We know that they had come into the district as a despised and feared class, but that on the whole the prejudice was overcome. We know what demanding and dangerous work the men did, and how hard the life was for the women. We know the conditions in which they lived, and that there were those concerned about their welfare, yet the railway people were constantly on the move. We know also that the Kettering to Manton line was part of the Midland Railway Company's plan, and that it was built in connection not only with the Melton to Nottingham line, but also far to the north the Settle & Carlisle, and to the south the access to London. So the work on this line had to keep in step with others, so they all more or less finished together. We know how the men worked over, under and along the route, and how the physical problems presented by the terrain were overcome. Indeed, by now we are probably pretty much in awe of what was being achieved. How the women coped I cannot think. But what we have not yet taken into account is a most important aspect, bearing in mind that the work was all in the open – the weather.

During the years when the railway was under construction, the weather endured not only by the railway people but by everyone living and working in the district was extraordinary, by any standards. It was regularly reported on by the press. Although the Welland valley was constantly named in these reports, the valleys of the Chater, Harper's Brook and the Ise were of course similarly affected, as were the other railway works in the region. My sources are the *Stamford Mercury* and the *Grantham Journal*.

1875

In July 1875, the month that the equipment, supplies and manpower began to be assembled, such torrential rain and heavy flooding occurred that the Welland valley suffered its worst inundation for many years. On the 14th and 15th it rained continuously for 36 hours. The river rose 6½ feet above average, and in many of the lower districts the engines had to be set to work to pump water out of the drains. Market Harborough and Stamford were badly affected, as were the villages along the valley, as well as the railway works. Also the temperature was very low, for a keen north-east wind blew incessantly. The wet weather continued until 14 August, when a dry period set in. September was a very fine month, with the temperature above average, but October was very stormy, with destructive gales, and above-average rainfall. Once again there was flooding throughout the country. Hundreds of acres were submerged in the Welland valley. In November, the month that work on Corby Tunnel began, thunderstorms, gales of great severity and floods caused the work to be suspended, and later in the month the greatest fall of rain ever known during any November caused more heavy flooding. In addition, the first heavy snows of the winter fell. Market Harborough, 6 or so miles from the source of the Welland, was badly affected by the floods, and at Stamford, a few miles downstream from where the line crosses the valley, the Market Hall was under several feet of water. To the north, blinding snowstorms and biting frosts, accompanied by gale-force winds, were reported at Melton Mowbray, thus affecting the other Midland line under construction.

1876

Things did not improve in 1876. Snowfalls and gales disrupted railway traffic and telegraph communications pretty well nationwide, and the district of the works was again badly hit in the first weeks of the year. That spring was the coldest and most stormy perhaps ever known. March was cold, very stormy and wintry; a gale raged continuously for 14 days, and the temperature for the month fell 7 degrees below freezing. Severe snowstorms disrupted telegraph communications again. Yet this was the month when the first brick was laid on the great viaduct. In April a short season of delightful weather caused hedges to burst forth and flowers to bloom; the temperature

on the 8th rose to 71 degrees in the shade. Then came a sudden change with storms of sleet and rain followed by bitter cold and heavy snowfall. On Good Friday, 14 April, a violent snowstorm, accompanied by a boisterous wind, caused such drifting that the highways were rendered impassable and the Great Northern rail traffic was brought to a halt in the district. The snow was swiftly followed by a rapid thaw, thus more flooding befell not only this region but further afield. During that week the weight of snow on the roof of Melton Mowbray station caused it partially to collapse. On 22 April the local press reported snowstorms in the Uppingham district as heavy as any other in the neighbourhood. Waggons, it was recorded, had been snowed up for several days, and the roads between Seaton station, Uppingham and Manton were completely blocked. There was loss of sheep and lambs, dying from suffocation in the drifts. But then another sudden and rapid thaw caused more disastrous floods.

During May bitterly cold north-east winds blew continuously for 14 days, but as the

In 1875 bad weather caused extensive flooding. This Edwardian postcard illustrates the problem in the Welland valley very well. *Doris Reynolds, Gretton Local History Society*

season progressed, the weather improved. June was very fair, and there was almost constant sunshine in July, and one Sunday was the hottest day for 30 years, resulting in cases of sunstroke. There was a very severe and damaging hailstorm towards the end of the month, though. In August violent thunderstorms, accompanied by torrential rain, were reported, and once again there was localised flooding. There followed a short period of weather favourable to the harvest, though excessive and unprecedented heat from the 12th to the 15th made harvesting very trying. September began and continued with rain – 5.24 inches were recorded that month. October was dry and fine and there were no further extremes of weather that year, except that December began with floods again, then became so mild that the *Grantham Journal* reported on a 'splendid bunch of primroses' gathered in Hambleton Woods (a mile or so from Manton station, these woods are now on the isthmus that juts into Rutland Water).

1877

However, in January 1877 heavy rain and melting snow caused floods again throughout the country. A few weeks later, in February, violent gales were reported, with heavy rain, snow, floods, and severe frosts all over the region, and the weather continued to be similarly harsh and arduous to the railway people and farmers alike, much as it had been in 1876.

From all over the country came reports in April of severe blizzards with roads and railway lines completely blocked, and telegraph services disrupted, just as occurred the year before. In the neighbourhood of the line heavy drifting created havoc and misery. Things did not improve markedly in May and June, when once again particularly violent thunderstorms brought widespread floods to the district. There was intense heat at the beginning of June, which caused 'several persons, principally exposed working men, to become ill and leave their work, but no fatal cases have been reported. The lightning on Monday night was truly

majestic, but no storm accompanied it.' July saw some improvement, but by August, the month of Rev and Mrs Barrett's wedding, more storms, heavy rain and hail brought distress to the farmers and navvies, and by November it was bitterly cold, and again, snow was falling. December continued in a similar fashion.

1878

In January 1878 heavy rain, preceded by snow, affected the region, but a change set in, and at the beginning of February severe frosts were reported, and skating was enjoyed on the frozen flood water on the meadows near Seaton. Then the weather became mild, and a period of fine weather with unusually high temperatures took place, and continued into March. But then, on 16 March, there was a sudden snowstorm preceded by a 'hurricane at Oakham, when it was with the greatest difficulty that the few pedestrians on the road maintained their perpendicular. These same persons, a few minutes afterwards, presented the appearance of walking mounds of snow.' In April snowstorms and wind storms were reported all over the country. As much as 9 inches of snow fell in some places, and once again railways were blocked and telecommunications interrupted. Yet that week the papers carried the report that the Midland's Melton Mowbray to Newark railway was nearing completion. In May thunderstorms of extraordinary severity passed over the neighbourhood, the heavy rain caused flooding again. In July, within days of the keying in of the last arch of the Welland Viaduct, severe storms hit Uppingham, and a house was struck by lightning in Orange Lane. In August there were violent thunderstorms, particularly in the Oakham area, with vivid lightning and torrential rain. On 1 November a heavy snowstorm was reported in Stamford, which seemed to have been general throughout the adjoining counties. In December there were again intense frosts for several days, and 'Market Harborough canal basin was crowded with skaters – candles stuck in lumps of snow gave the scene a most striking appearance.'

1879

The year of 1879 was spoken of as 'the worst season that has been known for very many years'. In January very hard weather resulted in almost the entire stoppage of work on the railways. This was commented on during the Midland Railway's Director's report included in another chapter. On 18 April snow 9 to 12 inches deep fell on Easter Day, followed by more heavy falls in the region. In May the weather continued very severe, with at least 10 degrees of frost prevailing at times. And in June the Whitsuntide weather was 'as dreary as had been the whole spring'. There was much concern for the depressed situation in agriculture, and in July special prayers were said for the weather to alleviate the distress. They must have been heard, for on 2 August the press recorded that 'The weather is at last everything that can be desired, the brightest sunshine having been appreciated for the past few days.' It was not to last – the following week there were reports of great thunderstorms, with floods causing railway difficulties. Windmills were wrecked by the powerful winds, and churches and animals in the fields were struck by lightning. There was a landslip on the Midland line near Leicester, and a horse in the station was killed by lightning.

Yet despite all this, amazingly, the Kettering to Manton line was finished on time, and opened on time, and the first train ran over the route on time. Once busy wooden villages had become empty and silent, and the turf huts disintegrated back into the hillsides.

The navvies had gone.

10
ACCIDENTS, ILLNESS AND DEATH

'No other class of working men follow their employment in such continual danger to life and limb as navvies. Few travellers reflect that each mile they pass over has cost a life or an accident.' So wrote Mrs Garnett. In many ways the railway works had all the harsh realities of frontier life: lonely communities isolated from established settlements inhabited by fiercely independent people. They had to rely to a large extent on their own resources as life's dramas of births, accidents, illnesses and deaths unfolded. Although Lucas & Aird, the Bishop's Mission and well-wishers had done much to provide for the religious, educational and social welfare of the railway people, I have found no evidence to suggest that any huts were set aside as makeshift hospitals on the Kettering to Manton line. Barrett wrote that no one knew other than those who saw it what the inconveniences of a crowded hut were for nursing purposes. Most of the seriously injured were taken to Stamford Infirmary, no doubt because of the rail link from Seaton. Some were taken to Kettering Cottage Hospital, and some to Leicester Infirmary. Terrible accidents happened, never mind the cause, and men suffered as much through, and died as a result of, the journey to the nearest hospital as from the incident itself. Imagine the agony, Mrs Garnett wrote, of being laid on some straw in a cart and jolted over country roads to the nearest station.

On 29 January 1876 the press reported:

'F. W. Browne, Esq, Uppingham, has been appointed surgeon to the new works which the Midland Railway Company are making from Manton to Kettering. Mr Brown has the care of the men from Manton to Gretton inclusive. Mr Browne has also been appointed medical officer for the ninth time to the Society of Oddfellows.'

Accidents on the works

When we consider the nature of the work it is not surprising that many accidents occurred, for the works involved men in great physical danger, with no health and safety guidelines to abide by. It seems that the men and their masters thought nothing of the very real perils all around them. The works was an unforgiving place, where tragedy struck with awful regularity. But tragedy did not seem to have a daunting effect. From contemporary writings it is clear that the men got used to the dangers, and took unnecessary, ridiculous risks, sometimes from bravado, sometimes from carelessness, often, it must be said, as a result of drink. Men worked at great heights and great depths. They dealt with unstable materials – earth, clay and rock. They toiled in water and mud, often in dreadful weather. They struggled with heavy barrows on slippery planks over sheer drops. They used unguarded machinery and were drawn into it. Horses took fright, braking systems failed – and sometimes accidents were simply accidental! What was true of public works in general, was also true of the Kettering to Manton railway.

From the newspapers of the day I have gleaned as much information as is available, but most of the accidents were simply not reported. This is obvious when making a comparison between parish archives and press reports. Even when they were recorded on the whole they lacked detail. A death was a death, and human effort was plentiful and cheap. Often when an inquest was held, the verdict shows that the blame was more often than not laid on the victim.

Many of the accidents involved falls, either from moving vehicles or from heights. Many more were the result of earth slips and rock falls. Some came about because scaffolding or platforms gave way, others because of carelessness or over-familiarity with machines. We have already seen death as a result of falls down shafts, of being trampled by a horse, and injuries through collapses of earth.

By July 1876 the Managing Committee of the Stamford & Rutland Infirmary was not happy! Although comparatively few reports of accidents had appeared in the press, it is clear that the numbers of cases admitted to Stamford Infirmary from the railway works had become a great strain on the resources.

The Mayor presided over the quarterly meeting:

'In consequence of the numerous cases of serious accidents sent from the railway works near Seaton, and the extra cost thereby entailed on the Infirmary, it was determined that in future 12s a week be charged for patients who are sent in through railway accidents. It was mentioned that a medical gentleman at Uppingham who has remitted these cases to the Infirmary received a large fund made up of 2d a week from every man engaged in the railway works in the district. The contractors for the works have forwarded a further donation of £5 on account of the six men who have been sent to the Infirmary with broken limbs.'

Accidents at the other end of the works included that of William Neal, who was

Remember Frederick Clarke Smith, whose horse took fright in a tunnel (Chapter 6)? He must have been a lad like this. There are several potential accidents in this picture: the man perched on the tip truck, the men working very close to the mechanical digger, the rudimentary braking system that caused William Hart's death (note the sprag projecting from the nearest waggon wheel), the possibility of an earth slip, and so on. *Newton Collection, courtesy of the Record Office for Leicestershire, Leicester and Rutland*

walking beside the line on his way home from his work as a ballast labourer at Glendon cutting on 26 May 1877 when a down express struck him. His injuries were severe and he was taken to the Cottage Hospital at Kettering, where no doubt he died. At Gretton a few months later two men were buried by Coroner's order on 15 October 1877. Their ages were unknown but one was called Samuel Smith and the other was Thomas Jones. They had been living in one of the Gretton huts, and were found dead together in a ditch, but how they came there and what they died of I have not discovered.

A 'guardian angel' may have hovered over the works in April 1878, when there was an incident that appears to be nothing short of miraculous. An unnamed workman fell from the viaduct at Seaton, a distance of some 70 feet, and 'singularly enough sustained no injury of importance. No bone was broken, and very little effect resulted from the shock to the system'. However, a few weeks later an inquest was opened one Friday evening at the Union Workhouse, Uppingham, upon the body of Patrick Duncan. He had not been so fortunate, for he was killed while working on the same viaduct. I did not find the report on the verdict, so I do not know how the accident occurred.

In May 1878 another inquest was held at Uppingham on a fatal accident that happened at Glaston. Twenty-one-year-old Edward William Hart was a fireman – that is to say a stoker on an engine – and was either inexperienced or did not take enough care. He had only been working for Lucas & Aird for about a month when he attempted to get up on the moving engine. But he slipped, and one of the trucks attached to the engine ran over his right leg, crushing it severely. He was taken to Leicester Infirmary, but 'mortification had set in', and he died a few days later.

There was another accident of quite a different kind that March, not far from where William Neal received his injuries nearly a year before:

'Early on Tuesday morning the driver of the mail train leaving Leicester at 1.52,

when approaching Kettering, saw two men lying on the Midland line, evidently having been knocked down by a passing train. Several men went to the spot and found the men were navvies who had been at work on the new railway in course of formation at Kettering. One had been dreadfully injured and was quite dead, while the other was half conscious. Restoratives were administered to the latter and he was conveyed to Leicester Infirmary, where he gave the name of Alfred Martin, 26, labourer. He stated he and his companion were on the line on Monday night, but how they were knocked down he is unable to state. Martin is in a critical condition.'

Then as now, there was a fascination in watching men at work and works in progress. In June 1876 a 74-year-old man called Thomas White was a spectator at the works near Corby Wood when he was knocked down by some ballast trucks and received severe injuries. Having been taken to Stamford Infirmary, he died within three hours of his reception. The account of the inquest gives an interesting glimpse into the events of that day, especially in the light of what was discussed earlier with regard to the transportation of an injured person, and the consequences of such a journey.

I omit the usual preamble and go straight to the evidence of Mr James Blackwell, who:

'...on the morning of the 28th June at about 10 o'clock, saw the deceased walking along the line on which a mortar wagon was travelling. He called to him to "look out", and the old man in trying to get out of the way fell just before the wagon reached him. He [the witness] ran and tried to stop it, but could not, and it struck the deceased on the thigh. Two or three men ran to his assistance, and they got the deceased from under the truck, one of the wheels of which was on his thigh. He was sensible, and they gave him some brandy. He was then taken in a cart to Rockingham Station, and thence to the Stamford Infirmary. Deceased had no business on the line – Mr Greenwood, house surgeon at the Infirmary, said deceased had been brought there about 1.30 in the omnibus from the Midland Station. He was in a state of collapse, from which he never rallied, and died at 3.30 from the shock. He had a fractured thigh. Jury returned the verdict of accidental death.'

As well as the spectacularly serious accidents, fatalities occurred through minor incidents that today we would brush aside, with the aid of antiseptics and antibiotics, clean rooms and dry beds. In those days a cut or a splinter could become septic, and, as Barrett said, apparently trifling wounds could develop into long and serious illnesses, ending frequently in death.

Accidents to working children and young people

Boys were employed on public works as young as 12 or 13, or as soon as they could do anything useful, and sadly many also died – as boys. One of the earliest fatal accidents concerning a working child on the railway was in May 1876. He was not named, and neither was the location where the incident occurred, but while greasing some tip trucks they were set in motion and passed over him, and he was killed. He was 11 years old. The following month Jacob Brown, aged 15, was run over by a wagon. He sustained a fractured skull, thigh and collar bone and was taken to Stamford Infirmary.

As a result of another fatal accident at Glaston, in December 1877, an inquest was held at Leicester Infirmary on the death of Alfred Hyde. He was the 13-year-old son of James Hyde, railway labourer, Wing, Rutland:

'It appeared from the evidence that the deceased was in the employment of Messrs Lucas and Aird, railway contractors. His duties were to attend the fire of an engine connected with the works, and on the 6th inst, while so employed, he got accidentally caught by a cog wheel and drawn into the engine.

The engine was stopped immediately, and it was then found that the lad's arm had been severed from his body. He was removed to Leicester Infirmary, where he died on Sunday. Mr Hetley, house surgeon, attributing death to the shock he sustained to his System. Verdict: accidental death.'

In October 1876 Albert Knight, a 17-year-old fireman on a portable engine, was on the engine when it was nearing an incline. Sprags of wood were used to block the wheels of the engine and trucks as a braking device, and these were kept on the front of the engine. Knight was on the engine arranging the sprags so the brakeman could take them to stop the wheels when he fell off, and a wheel went over his body. He was taken home, and the doctor was sent for, and he was taken to the Infirmary where he died of mortification to the left leg. Verdict: accidental death.

Illness: a local and national concern

In addition to death by accident, there was of course death by illness. The press carried reports of outbreaks of smallpox both in the region and nationally during those years. There were also cases of typhoid, cholera, hydrophobia, diphtheria, and scarlet fever. What we now tend to dismiss as 'childhood diseases' were then deadly plagues, and occurred regularly. From what we have seen in regard to the living conditions and the weather endured by millions of people, much of what follows comes as no surprise. Yet we take so much of modern life and the benefits it brings for granted.

This is the national report published on 10 November 1876:

'THE DISEASES THAT KILL – The Registrar-General shows, in the report which he has just issued on the year 1874, that two-thirds of the deaths in England occurred from one or other of 15 causes. Bronchitis heads the list: it caused 53,022 deaths, a larger number than in any year included in a table extending over the preceding 15 years. Next come phthisis, or consumption, which cuts short 49,379 lives, a smaller number than any of the preceding years. Atrophy and debility account for 30,995 deaths, chiefly of young children. Old age, which should be highest on the list of causes of death, is fourth, and to it 28,604 deaths are referred; the list includes 12,495 men and 16,109 women, all over 65 years old, and some centenarians. Heart disease, which continues to increase, accounts for 28,513 deaths; and convulsions caused 27,139, almost all of them children. Pneumonia, more fatal than for some few years since, occasioned 25,027 deaths. Eighth on the list stands scarlet fever, to which as many as 24,922 deaths are attributed; an epidemic of scarlet fever had set in, and this number is nearly double that of either of the two next preceding years. Diarrhoea, which is more fatal than it was 20 years ago, caused 21,204 deaths, more than 18,000 of them occurring among children under five years of age.'

That was the national picture. Here is part of the report published in July 1876 from the Local Board of the Stamford, Rutland & General Infirmary, to give it its full title:

'Mr Howard, Medical Officer of Health for the Borough ... reported 2 or 3 cases of enteric fever, and a few cases of scarlet fever, many cases of severely inflamed throats, some complicated with quinsy. During the last month many cases of chicken pox in children have occurred. On former occasions I have observed that chicken-pox is often a forerunner of smallpox and though I have little fear of the latter disease spreading in this borough, if it should be introduced from any other locality where it is prevalent, because most of our population is well protected by vaccination, yet I think the authority should bear in mind that you possess no proper hospital accommodation for the treatment of the disease if it should come to us in the person of a tramp or any traveller.'

Although mention is made of the protection afforded by vaccination, and although it was an obligation of law, cases were constantly published in the local press of parents being prosecuted for not having their children vaccinated. And as for concern about a tramp or traveller introducing disease, clearly it was valid. They were coming in droves. Hundreds were in the district already, with more arriving daily, drawn by the various public works in progress. The roaming habits of the navvies must have rendered almost impossible a systematic vaccination programme. Much anxiety was expressed by medical officers and sanitary inspectors regarding the rising incidence of smallpox, fever cases and other infectious illnesses, with no isolation hospitals either at Stamford or Kettering.

Only a few weeks before, on 26 March 1876, there was a report of the appointment of a Special Committee at Stamford to consider the propriety of providing additional buildings for the reception of infectious cases. Strong objection was raised in the town to bringing in such cases from the surrounding district. Reference was made to the numerous cases of fever in Stamford and the surrounding villages the previous winter, and it was particularly stressed that there was no intention to receive smallpox cases. Far to the north, in May 1871, an epidemic of smallpox had broken out on the works of the Settle to Carlisle railway, and 80 people died. Many of the workers came south to Rutland, Northamptonshire and Leicestershire to the new railway works; they did not bring the disease with them, but it must have been a risk of which the townspeople were well aware.

In October 1875, at Uppingham, right on the doorstep of the Kettering to Manton line, typhoid fever broke out, and the School was absent for three months. It returned in January, following official assurances that all that modern science could do to make the school houses healthy had been done. Nevertheless, after three weeks the fever returned. On 23 March 1876 the entire school was transferred to Borth near Aberystwyth, where it remained for a whole year, and became 'Uppingham by the Sea', while the town of Uppingham was put in order.

Illness among the railway people

I have found no evidence of the epidemics that visited the surrounding district breaking out in the hut settlements of the Kettering to Manton line, but there was certainly a lot of illness. The navvies worked in the wet, came in wet, probably slept on damp beds, and their clothes never properly dried out. The causes of most of the deaths brought about by illness, and there were many, were those associated with crowded conditions and working out of doors in all weathers.

Referring to illness and the cramped circumstances in some of the huts, Barrett wrote: 'Whilst speaking of population, I remember one case in which the occupants of a hut numbered nineteen souls; father, mother, seven children and ten lodgers. The lodgers were dismissed, and the disease was stayed before it ended in any mortality.' It was almost as a by-line that he mentioned the disease to be scarlatina. The main thing was that it was contained.

Parish registers reveal the many deaths that occurred in the huts all along the line, from mothers, young babies and children, to men in their prime and some quite elderly. But they are not very forthcoming when it comes to details, and few of the deaths on the works from illness reached the newspapers. One that did told a very sad story, while at the same time it revealed a lot about the character and death of one young miner at Glaston. The inquest was reported on 1 December 1877:

'On Saturday afternoon, an enquiry was held into the circumstances connected with the death of Charles Brickenborough, a young miner, aged 27. The deceased first complained of illness on Saturday week, but worked up till Monday night. On Tuesday he visited the doctor, yet was not apparently taken seriously ill until an hour and a half before his death, about 3.30am

on Saturday last. In fact he walked about daily. He lodged with Mr Masters, inspector, who summoned Dr Browne as soon as he apprehended danger. A verdict of "heart disease, combined with pulmonary infection", was returned. The young man was of exemplary character, and had regularly forwarded to his widowed mother a sovereign monthly. The Coroner, Dr Browne, and the jury made a subscription for the bereaved mother, which will be supplemented by a collection made voluntarily by his fellow workmen, who followed him to his last resting place in respectable numbers.'

This report not only tells us the circumstances of this young man's courage in the face of a fatal illness, and of his character; it also illustrates some points made by other contemporary writers. Navvies were never buried as paupers. They tended their own sick and buried their own dead. The contractor gave the coffin, and a respectable internment was provided, attended by as many men who could be spared. Most of the accounts of navvy funerals I have come across end with words to the effect of 'He was followed to his last resting place by respectable numbers'.

Barrett recalled a young Kentish navvy dying at Seaton huts. When he died, another Kentish man searched the works for other men of Kent to bear him to his grave. After any navvy funeral, the more drinking that went on the more complementary it was to the departed, once he was safely buried. The navvies were noted for being generous to the families of killed or injured workmates. Again, one of Barrett's recollections was of the death of a man he referred to as 'poor S——', who was killed by a fall down one of the shafts. He wrote very touchingly of the men's honest sympathy as their mate lay dying by the hut door, and of how they collected more than £80 for his widow and children, an enormous sum by the standards of today. I am sure this poor man was John Stone, the account of whose fatal fall is found in Chapter 5.

Life on the works was, then, harsh and dangerous, and accidents and illness claimed lives and limbs. Barrett wrote of the need for a hospital on site; of navvies sitting up night after night as they tended a sick work-mate, although they had been hard at work all day; of the dead lying under a sheet in the corner of a hut, because there was nowhere to take them. He wrote of many acts of kindness shown one to another. Williams also picked this up, and went on to say that ignorant and violent as some of them were, they were open-handed with their comrades, and would share their last penny with their friends who were in distress. They also had a shrewdness, he said, which got many a one in a scrape and many another out. But they did get drunk, and there were wild incidents.

Stamford got its accommodation for infectious diseases as a result of the recommendations of the Special Committee. In August 1877 the Marquis of Exeter was invited to lay the foundation stone for the new wards for the reception of infectious diseases, and in 1879 the new block was opened.

11
CRIME, COURTS AND THE COMMUNITY

'The rich man in his castle,
The poor man at his gate,
God made them, high or lowly,
And ordered their estate.'
Cecil Frances Alexander

This was and is a district of small communities, of plough and pasture, of pheasants and foxes. The squire in the big house, the parson in the vicarage, the doctor and the schoolmaster, each had his sphere of power and influence. Everyone had their place. Everyone knew their place. Here was the 'natural order' of things, operating as it had from centuries past. It was not only the way things were, it was the way they had always been. But it was not the idyllic life portrayed so romantically by many artists and poets of the day. The dreadful poverty and all that poverty brought in its train existed in the rural villages in the vicinity of the Kettering to Manton line as it did elsewhere. Nevertheless, the communities carried on, in the shadow of the church and the 'big house', as they had done time out of mind. Then came all those strangers, and the status quo was tipped on its head.

We have considered the effect the coming of the railway builders had on the local population, and how their life of necessity set the navvy families apart. An article entitled 'Work Among Navvies' in *The Sunday Magazine* of 1888 illustrates this. It not only underlines many of the points already made in this book, but also leads very neatly towards this section:

'It is strange now and then to turn off the high-roads of our civilisation and to find a whole class of people living close to a most elaborate system of law and order, and yet outside it all, like the wandering population of our canal-boats and the great army of our navvies. They are simply and literally outside everything – outside the school, outside the parish, outside the circle which has the chapel for its centre. Among them there is no sanitary system, and in the villages which they put up and pull down within a few months, the ordinary laws about the sale of drink are practically unknown. They might be pioneers of civilisation in the wilderness rather than toilers in the midst of cultivation, wealth, and luxury.'

There were of course many reports of crime involving the navvies of the Kettering to Manton line, especially during the latter months of 1875 and 1876. During the time of the railway's construction crimes reported include drunkenness, the taking of game, trespass, stealing, assault, sleeping rough, hawking without a licence, damage to property, a serious case of rape, a case of sheep stealing, and a case of manslaughter.

Police, penalties and Parliament

In 1856 a Police Act was passed in Parliament making it obligatory for all counties to raise and maintain a constabulary force, and as a result serious crimes against property fell steeply, as did crimes of violence. A professional police force was thus recognised as an important means of crime prevention. But locally, the sheer numbers of incomers arriving daily threatened to swamp the existing forces of law and order. Something had to be done, and in its edition of 5 November 1875 the *Stamford Mercury* announced:

'RUTLAND: we are glad to observe that, in compliance with a requisition, numerously signed and presented to the magistrates, they have agreed to appoint three additional police-constables to act between Manton Station and Harringworth, where the new railway works are in progress in the county.'

A similar arrangement was made on the Northamptonshire side.

Individual policemen were occasionally named in the newspaper reports of navvies breaking the law. Superintendent Murfitt went to London to apprehend Elizabeth Wells. Inspector Barwell and Sergeant Wilson were involved in the only case of sheep-stealing that I came across. PC Woodcock was involved in a serious affray at Stamford, in which some Kettering and Manton navvies were implicated. PC Evans went to Bedford to apprehend Eliza Daniels. He was also injured in an affray at Barrowden on 13 May 1876, where he sustained such serious injuries that he was suspended from duty. PC Martin was very active in the Seaton area, as was PC Brown. PC Wheely was continually getting himself assaulted at Wing. PC Davies was seriously wounded in a desperate assault committed at the railway huts near Kettering, which arose through a dispute between the navvies and their foreman about wages. On another occasion he sustained severe wounds to his head and face when he disturbed three men sleeping rough in an outhouse. SPC (later PC) Dunford, like PC Wheely, was always getting himself beaten up in the Wing and Glaston area. Police Sergeant Meadows and PC Jesse Fennimore operated in the Gretton and Corby district; the most notable case with which they were associated was the suspected murder at the tunnel. We will look in more detail at some of these cases as this chapter progresses.

The police, when faced with a group of hostile navvies, were outnumbered and vulnerable, no matter how courageous they were. Such incidents were regularly reported in the press. For example, in the *Stamford Mercury* of 11 February 1876, in the account of proceedings at Oakham Petty Sessions, we read that Fred Atkins, Henry Clarke, John Goiner and William Millward, all of Seaton, railway labourers, had been summoned for assaulting and resisting the police at Bisbrooke. Atkins and Clarke were fined £1 each with costs, and Goiner and Millward, who did not appear, were each committed for 14 days hard labour. The police concerned were not named in this report. In the *Grantham Journal* of 13 May 1876, under the Uppingham Police we find that John Taylor, John Lusted and William Phillips, railway workers, had been charged with damaging windows and doors at Barrowden. There had been what the paper described as 'the usual fight', when PC Evans sustained such injuries that it was expected he would be unfit for duty for some time to come. The sentence was 28 days hard labour. On 22 May 1876 William Ham and Samuel Hayden, both miners at Wing, were committed for six weeks hard labour for assaulting PC Dunford. There were many other similar cases.

As I gathered material for this chapter, I vaguely thought 'hard labour' meant stone-breaking or road-building. Then it occurred to me that the navvies were employed in doing similar work all day long, so I began to look into the Victorian penal system. I found that it could be described in one word – savage. Hard labour meant pointless unproductive drudgery, such as revolving a treadmill, designed so as to give maximum strain on the body of the unfortunate prisoner. Or it could mean cranking a barrel full of gravel or other heavy substance for so many thousand revolutions, cunningly calculated by a device invented for the purpose, before the hapless inmate had 'earned' his meagre meal. This hard labour did not achieve any useful purpose, for instance to produce power or pump water – it was purely and simply to induce the utmost exhaustion and degradation. It did not even act as a deterrent, for have I found many instances of prisoners re-offending.

Poaching had always been a serious matter, incurring savage punishments that had prevailed since feudal times. During the 19th century successive Acts of Parliament modified the Game Laws. For example, until 1816 any person found to be armed at night, and trespassing in search of game, was liable on conviction to a sentence of death. The Act of 1816 changed this to seven years transportation. However, we should not construe this as being lenient, for to all intents and purposes it was virtually a life sentence, dispatching as it did the convicted man to the other end of the earth, away from wife and children, home and hearth. Generally speaking, even if he survived the perils of the long sea journey, the harsh conditions of the penal colony, and reached the end of his sentence in reasonable health, he would be unlikely to be able to gather the means together to make his way back again. Poachers could still be put to death as late as 1828, and we may do well to remember that the last public execution took place in London in 1868. The extreme penalty of transportation for seven years was not abolished until 1867, less than ten years before the railway workers came to build the Kettering to Manton line.

Various Acts of Parliament made a distinction between different kinds of game. For instance, the Night Poaching Act of 1828 distinguished between game birds, their eggs, and hares. Rabbits came under another category. Rabbits had to be taken or killed to constitute an offence, and to prosecute a poacher for trespass in search of game under this Act it was necessary to prove he had in his possession guns, nets, snares, etc.

In 1827 spring-guns and man-traps were prohibited as an attempt to deter poaching. These vile instruments were positively medieval in their cruelty. They were widely advertised, not only as articles for sale, but also that they were employed on certain estates. This was supposed to warn off prospective poachers. Should the unfortunate miscreant fall foul of the hidden devices, the advertisements frequently carried this disclaimer: 'Anyone maimed or killed had only himself to blame'. But 'villainous poachers' were not the only victims:

respectable and innocent people were often injured by them. Inanimate machines, they were indiscriminate in their effect. In the case of the man-trap, it not only caused excruciating pain and injury, but was also likely to maim for life, and was virtually impossible to escape from unaided.

The spring-gun was as likely to kill as to maim, and was just as liable to be triggered by an innocent person stumbling over a trip-wire as a poacher intent on illegal purpose. Also, a spring-gun could and often did injure more than one person at a time, since the trip-wire was designed to fire off a charge of ball or shot, which spread with terrible consequences. Although rendered illegal by the Act of 1827, the use of man-traps and spring-guns continued in some of the more remote areas, where times were slow to change. By the Poaching Prevention Act of 1862, those animals and birds classed as game, and the eggs that were protected under the law, were again clearly defined. In addition, this Act gave powers of search to any constable or police officer, on any highway, street or public place, should there be good grounds for suspicion.

Poachers, landowners and gamekeepers

Perhaps one of the most prevailing images handed down to us regarding the railway navvies is that they were not only all drunken rioters, but were also all prone to poaching. Gangs of navvies, we are led to believe, their lurcher dogs, their terriers, guns and nets, foraged about the hedgerows and woods to the peril of the game and the terror of the neighbourhood. This was well illustrated in one of the first articles to appear in the local press regarding the new works, and was quoted in full in an earlier chapter. Of particular significance here are the remarks regarding game and the game laws: 'They have, however, no respect for the provisions of the game laws, considering, as they say, that game is made for those as can catch it.' A few weeks after the works began, the Rutland Petty Sessions were held at Oakham, and on 4 October 1875 the first case to involve

Kettering to Manton navvies was heard. William Cunnington and George Wyman, employed as railway workers at Seaton, were tried for trespassing in search of game. They were found guilty, and fined £1 4s 7d each, including costs.

Admittedly, while the railway was under construction many cases of poaching reported in the press did involve railway workers. But when we consider the hundreds who came to live and work in the region, a district as famous for its game as its foxes, the numbers brought before the local benches of magistrates were comparatively few. From the accounts I have read, it seems to me there were no more cases that concerned navvies than those that involved villagers, yet the railway population far outnumbered the locals.

George Wyman was not deterred by the heavy fine imposed upon him in October 1875, for he appeared before the court again on 1 April the following year, when he was described as 'railway labourer, Seaton'. On this occasion he was charged with assaulting Police Constables Martin and Brown at Bisbrooke. He was found guilty and was committed to gaol for 28 days. The circumstances of the assault were not reported by the newspaper. On the same day, at the same court, William Cheshire, Henry Mattson, Charles March, John Moore alias Allen, John Gowers, alias Cockney, John Brown and Aaron Arnold, all referred to as navvies working at Glaston, were charged with using guns and dogs for the purpose of taking game, on Sunday 19th ult. They were found guilty and fined £2 with 2s 5d costs each – in other words more than a week's wages.

Although this group of navvy-poachers would probably be thought of today as a gang, poaching in gangs in the late 19th century came under a different category of crime. It usually referred to professional poachers, men who were organised and operated together to make a living by selling the game. Turnpikes and railways gave easy access from the country to the towns, where there was a ready market with no questions asked. In a similar way the motorway network of the early 21st century facilitates much crime today.

It is more than likely that William Cheshire

and company were enjoying a spring Sunday afternoon of sport, with the anticipation of a good chance of augmenting their food supply with fresh meat for themselves and their hut-mates. They may also have found the thrill of evading the law enticing. But poaching was illegal. They had committed a crime, and it was a crime that carried with it heavy penalties, as we have seen. Yet somehow it was not considered by the labouring classes as morally wrong. In evidence given before the Select Committee on Game Laws in May 1873, it was brought to the attention of the Committee that 'it was very difficult for labourers to believe that hares and rabbits belonged to any individual; they were surely to be regarded as wild animals and the fair property of anybody skilful enough to take them' – a sentiment earlier expressed in the quotation from the newspaper, that game is made for those as can catch it. But of course the landowners thought otherwise, and the landowners were frequently magistrates.

Fines were heavy on a convicted poacher, and amounted to the best part of or more than a week's wage, as we saw earlier. And so when 'Welsh Jimmy' and David Edwards of Glaston Railway Huts appeared before Rutland Petty Sessions in March 1878, they were each fined 20 shillings with costs for game trespass. At Kettering Petty Sessions in the same month, John Williams, navvy, was charged with using snares to take game at Rushton, and was fined 10 shillings and 9s 11d costs. Although among the rural poor there was the widely held opinion that the poacher was morally innocent, nevertheless he was a criminal in the eyes of the law and was dealt with accordingly.

Landowners, then as now, went to great expense to establish their game reserves. Game was valuable property, and the landowners employed gamekeepers to protect it. The role of the gamekeeper was not only to raise great quantities of partridges, pheasants and so on for sport, but to protect it from hazards, both natural and the attacks of poachers. He had to rear a good stock of game, keep it well fed during the closed season to prevent it from straying away from the estate, and kill the vermin that was a threat to eggs and young birds. He was also the first line of defence against determined and often hungry men, as described in this newspaper advertisement: '...he must be accustomed to all the tricks of the Poachers, and must not be afraid of them, he must be strong, active, hardy, sober, and honest, and have an undeniable character from his last place...' Gamekeepers had good knowledge of the local villains, but with the coming of the railway workers they were faced with brawny strangers, who were not only determined but also had the advantage of anonymity.

The required qualities of courage and strength were called upon one Sunday afternoon in February 1876 when Mr John Kyle and his assistant were on duty on the estate of the Duke of Buccleuch, near Kettering, who was one of the principal landowners on the Northamptonshire side of the works. Mr Kyle and his unnamed assistant came upon a group of navvies poaching in a field near the huts erected by the crossroads at Rushton. Mr Kyle demanded the nets, etc, from them, but the navvies made a savage attack upon him. He was struck on the head with a spade, and among other injuries he sustained was a broken jaw. There was no clue to the identity of the ruffians, the press said. How Mr Kyle recovered was not reported. That he recovered at all is remarkable in the light of the medical resources of the day. This was the most violent poaching affray to involve the Kettering to Manton navvies that I found in the local press. But I make the point that despite their reputation, not all navvies were poachers, not all poachers were apprehended, and not all cases were reported.

And not all those charged were convicted. One such case appeared in the *Stamford Mercury* on 21 September 1877, and because it is so unusual the report is quoted here in full:

'KETTERING PETTY SESSIONS: William Hawes, navvy, of Corby, was charged with stealing two guns at Corby. Prosecutor, a gamekeeper to Lady Cardigan, deposed that on the 4th inst he went to Clough's public house at Corby. Defendant and several other navvies were there. In a few minutes he left the house and went on to the road to meet the carrier who brought a gun from Kettering. He was carrying a gun. Hearing someone behind him he turned round and saw the prisoner, who said he should have the gun. They had a struggle, and both fell to the ground. While they were down one of the prisoner's companions came up and kicked the witness. For the defence an alibi was set up. Several witnesses said the prisoner was at the huts at the time of the occurrence, and he was discharged.'

While not strictly speaking 'poaching', the following case is included in this section, and concerns the only instance of sheep or cattle stealing by navvies on the line. The *Stamford Mercury* of 7 July 1876, while recording proceedings of the Northamptonshire sessions, reported the case. Samuel Rivvett, 24, and John Ward, 29, navvies, were indicted for killing a sheep with intent to steal a portion, the property of Mr Charles Richards at Glendon, on 5 June. Mr Jacques was the prosecutor. In evidence it was said that the Midland Railway Company are widening a portion of their line on the prosecutor's farm, and the prisoners had access to a field in which there was a flock of sheep, which were safe at half past six on the evening in question, but next morning it was found that one of them had been killed and the legs removed before being skinned. The liver and heart had also been taken out. Inspector Barwell went with Sergeant Wilson to the Crispin beerhouse, and traced the missing legs to the prisoners' possession. They were found guilty and sentenced to 12 months hard labour each.

Of rabbits, pigeons, turnips and apples

The penalties for what we may consider now to be less serious crimes were very severe in those days. For example:

For stealing growing turnips:
                    10 shillings plus costs
For stealing a quantity of apples:
                    7 days hard labour

For stealing two rabbits: 14 days hard labour
For stealing clothing: 6 months hard labour
For stealing a 9-gallon cask of beer:
                                6 weeks hard labour
For stealing 24 pigeons: 28 days hard labour

I have concluded that these reflect the attitude the magistrates had towards the navvies, and their attempt to control them, because similar offences committed by local villagers do not appear to have been dealt with so rigorously. You must take my word for this, because I did not extract examples to illustrate the point.

The following account by an unnamed reporter for the *Grantham Journal* contains such detail that we might be witnesses to the crime committed by a Kettering to Manton navvy in Uppingham one December day in 1875:

'A somewhat exciting event occurred in Uppingham High Street. It appeared that a woman, who was outside Mr Catlin's shop, saw a navvy take two rabbits from hooks in the window, deliberately put them in his pocket, and walk off. She very properly rang the bell and called Mr Catlin's attention to the fact, and he went in pursuit. Coming up with the fellow, he accosted him, and accused him of the theft, and received in return a blow over the head, with one of the rabbits. With assistance, he took away the rabbit, and for a short time held his man, but he escaped and ran down to the east end of the town, before he was captured and brought to the Market Place, where, upon the entreaties of his friends he was released, only to be caught for a third and fourth time. He was handed over to the police. A desperate resistance followed, but he was lodged in the lock-up, and on Monday brought before the Rev the Chancellor Wales, and remanded until the next Petty Sessions.' (*Grantham Journal*, 11 December 1875)

After such a detailed article, it was something of an anticlimax when I found the outcome in the issue of 28 January: 'Charles Warner, a navvy, was charged with stealing two rabbits, and sentenced to 14 days hard labour.' A similar case was heard at Kettering Petty Sessions, in June 1877, when George Edwards, a tramping brick-maker, pleaded guilty of stealing 8 pounds of beef, the property of Mr Isaac Gibson, Corby, and was committed to three weeks hard labour.

The case of the 24 pigeons is an interesting one. Morcott, though not directly on the Kettering to Manton route, was one of several villages where navvies lodged. This report appeared in the *Journal* under Uppingham Police, and once again we have a very graphic account:

'Joseph Taylor, Morcott, and Charles Brown, Coventry, navvies, were charged by Mr F. Swift of Morcott, with breaking into his dovecote on 17th September 1876, and stealing 2 dozen pigeons. It appears that both prisoners lodged at J. Barfield's, Morcott. On Monday morning, the 18th, PC Evans, who was investigating the robbery, met the prisoner Taylor in the street. He appeared very lame, and on being questioned said that he fell downstairs on Saturday night. Superintendent Murfitt on receiving information of the robbery, proceeded to Morcott and searched Barfield's house. Taylor was apprehended, and pigeon feathers and down were found in his pockets. He was also considerably injured in the wrist and groin, which he admitted had been done by falling from near the top of the dovecote while getting the pigeons. Brown was afterwards apprehended in the cutting at Glaston. The pigeons were stewed for dinner on Sunday. The prisoner Brown said he had plucked them all, Taylor being hurt so much he had to go to bed directly...'

The prisoners were remanded to the Petty Sessions, and sentenced to 28 days hard labour.

There was quite a lot of crime against the local community, especially in the autumns when fields of vegetables and ripening orchards tempted the men to steal. Many such cases were reported all along the line. For example, George Anderson and Henry Wollett, both of Chipping Norton and both navvies, were charged with stealing growing apples at Glaston, the property of J. W. Kington, in September 1876. They were each fined £1 and committed for 14 days hard labour. Charles Brown, navvy, Seaton (not the pigeon man) was fined 15 shillings for stealing a quantity of apples and growing turnips, the property of Mr Royce, Seaton. George Doughty, labourer on the railway works, received a sentence of seven days hard labour for stealing growing apples. Henry Clarke, brick-maker, was fined 10 shillings with 8 shillings costs for stealing growing turnips. William Newton, navvy, Rushton, was fined 10 shillings plus 16 shillings costs for stealing potatoes from a field at Rushton. There were many other similar incidents.

'No visible means of support'

William Robinson and Charles Brown, navvies, were committed to seven days hard labour for lodging in an outhouse at Seaton without visible means of support. Thomas Stones and Thomas Spake, navvies, were committed for 21 days hard labour for sleeping in a haystack. William Thorn and James Wills were committed for three weeks hard labour for being in an outhouse for unlawful purpose. George Lee of Leicester and John Green of Westminster were charged with a similar offence and committed for 10 days hard labour. Others were charged with sleeping under a hedge; still others with lying in a ditch. And so it went on … but we must not necessarily assume that because a man was tramping the roads and sleeping rough he was by definition a ne'er-do-well, although indeed he might have been one. We have seen in earlier chapters how men walked long distances seeking employment. Mrs Garnett suggested that men used to the outdoor life, who had tramped a considerable distance, would rather sleep with no roof, preferring a rough doss under a haystack to the dirt and companions of a low lodging house. But it was illegal, and was dealt with accordingly.

Sometimes one thing led to another, and sleeping rough led to a more serious incident. One of the most dreadful assaults on a policeman by a navvy working on the line occurred at Kettering, when two men were found in an outhouse for unlawful purpose. Joseph Althorpe, alias 'Flinkey', with another man, was found by PC Davies. On his disturbing them, as the *Mercury* put it, one man went away, but the prisoner fell foul of the constable, overpowered him, and inflicted severe wounds upon his head and face. Evidence was given about the extent of the injuries and how they were probably done. The constable had to sit throughout the trial, and it was noted what a weak state he was in. Unfortunately I do not appear to have noted the outcome.

Disputes with the Company

It will be remembered that in an earlier chapter legal land purchase procedures were considered. Despite the statutes in place to cover this, the Midland Railway Company itself fell foul of the law on several occasions. In December 1875 an enquiry was held at Glaston before two Justices of the Peace regarding the temporary occupation of land by the Company for building the line. It appeared from the evidence that the Company had taken possession of 9 acres of capital feeding land, part of a farm of mixed quality, held by Mr Thomas Stokes and Lord Lonsdale, without previously giving the notice required by the statute. The following account is compiled from *Stamford Mercury* and *Grantham Journal* articles.

At the Sheriff's Court, Uppingham, on 12 April 1876, before Mr Graham, Assessor, and a jury, the case of the Earl of Lonsdale v the Midland Railway Company was heard. Mr Brown and Mr Wright were council for Lord Lonsdale, and Mr Bennett and Mr Paine were council for the railway company. It was explained that the Earl claimed compensation not only for the 9 acres of land taken by the Company, but also for damage by severance and injury to a fox covert, which had been rendered most dangerous owing to the new line running close by, and the mouth of the long tunnel within a few yards of it. There was long and detailed consideration of the estimated value of various aspects of the property by land agents and surveyors. Mr Fabling and Mr West, Lord Lonsdale's huntsmen, also gave evidence regarding the danger and damage to the fox covert. Mr Stokes, the tenant farmer, proved the rental value of the land. The learned Assessor having summed up, the jury gave a verdict for £2,100 15s, made up as follows: 9 acres of land and timber thereon, £956 5s, severance £554 10s, fox covert £500, hedges and gates £100.

By 1878 the Company, authorised by the Midland Railway (Additional Powers) Act of 1874, had purchased all the land it needed to build the railway. Mrs Elizabeth Goodhall had previously sold more than 38 acres of her land in the parish of Gretton. Subsequently about 5 acres of this, needed for the tunnel, were acquired by the Company. But it was not until 1890, after Mrs Goodhall's death, when her son and heir Colonel Goodhall was due to inherit, that it was found an error had been made. The land had not been legally sold to the Midland Company at all, since the person from whom it was bought was not a freeholder. However, there was no question that the Company had acquired the land by devious means – there had been a genuine though serious mistake. There was an amicable settlement, and Colonel Goodhall received his inheritance.

Troubles at the huts

Drink was sold in the 'shants', and in many of the huts. This was considered by the landlords to be a good source of income, but the sale of drink led to exploitation and the obvious problems that went with it. Mrs Garnett, when writing of the reservoir navvies in the North, said that gangers who were 'drink-selling hut-keepers' frequently turned away men who would not drink, and drink was sold to men who were not their lodgers. In her writings, considering that she was a stalwart worker in the Temperance movement, Mrs Garnett was surprisingly sympathetic towards the reasons why the navvies drank. Naturally she did not approve, though. Cold, hungry

and tired, a man on the tramp had every temptation to drink, she wrote. The hard working conditions and subsequent exhaustion, especially when men were on piecework, was another reason why they drank themselves into oblivion when their day's toil was done. If a man said he had made 'thirteen days in a week', who can wonder at the strain on his powerful physique, Mrs Garnett pointed out.

It was the same situation on the Kettering to Manton works. The tough life, with men coming and going, the overcrowding of men who were often strangers to each other, and the ready access to strong drink, led to much drunkenness, fights, theft, and so on. The 'shants' and the hut settlements were set up by the contractors, and the shanty-keepers were on the whole respectable men. Many of the families taking in lodgers were respectable too. But crimes were committed in the settlements, and the 'shants' were the most frequent places where they occurred. Incidentally, the press frequently referred to a 'shant' as a canteen, another word that has modified its meaning – it seems that 'shant' and 'canteen' were interchangeable in those days. Of all the huts along the Kettering to Manton works, we return to the 'shant' at Seaton for some of the anecdotes in this section, but that is not to suggest that this was any worse or any better than others along the line. You will remember that in Chapter 5 we visited this 'shant' one February night, when a crime was committed.

The year 1876 was an eventful one. The line was making great progress, the workforce was pretty well at full strength along the whole works, and many crimes took place. Walter, or Wallace, Read, navvy, of the 'shant', Seaton, was charged with stealing two pairs of trousers, two vests, three handkerchiefs, and 15 French pennies from the Three Horseshoes Inn, Seaton. He pleaded guilty and was sent for 21 days hard labour. This was one of the earliest reports concerning a man who lived at the Seaton 'shant'. On 30 June 1876 Alfred Bradley, sawyer, was charged by Thomas Oxenham with stealing a pair of boots, a pair of leather leggings, a carpet bag, two print shirts and two woollen shirts. According to the press he had been engaged as a servant in the canteen for a few days, absconded, and was found in possession of the property at Medbourne, a few miles from Seaton. At the Rutland Assizes he was sentenced to six months imprisonment with hard labour.

Fortunately for research purposes the shanty-keeper at Seaton had an unusual surname: Oxenham. In the Ginger White case, related in Chapter 5, Thomas Oxenham himself said in evidence that he 'kept the Shant at Seaton to accommodate 40 men'. Thomas Henry Oxenham was a married man; his wife's name was Sarah, and they had at least three children. I first noticed this couple in the Harringworth Baptism Register, when, in March 1876, their daughter Caroline had been baptised. They were given as living at Seaton, and Thomas's occupation was registered as shopkeeper. That does not necessarily mean to say that he was not then at the 'shant', for as well as lodgings, stores and drink were sold there. His name occurs in Seaton reports several times, and I have presumed that he was there at the 'shant' from start to finish. Another child, Ernest William, was baptised, and his father's occupation was recorded then as canteen proprietor. Sadly, like so many infants in those days, the baby appears in the Seaton Burial Register: '7th April 1878 Ernest William Oxenham 11 months Seaton Railway Canteen'.

There were many cases of drunkenness and fighting in the streets of Uppingham, Barrowden, Corby, Stamford and Kettering, as well as in the settlements. Thomas Oxenham himself was assaulted by John Davies in August. Wilful damage to property, belonging both to the Company and to members of the community was regularly reported, as was theft. John Williams, alias Soldier, railway labourer, stole half-a-crown, one shilling and six pence from the canteen at Seaton, and there was the theft by Edward Evans, Worcester, of a slop or smock belonging to Henry Jones, also at the canteen, Seaton, valued at 5 shillings. He was committed for 14 days hard labour.

It was not only the men who committed crime. In February that year we learn from the *Stamford Mercury* that Eliza Daniels, 18, was charged at Uppingham with stealing a sovereign and a bonnet, the property of David Page, one of the engine drivers at Wing. It appears that David Page and his wife kept a hut at Wing, and there the prisoner and a navvy named Lawrence Taylor went to live on 27 January, making out they were man and wife. On the following Monday Mrs Page missed a sovereign, and told Eliza of the loss, who remarked that the children must have taken it. The next day she left the hut, and in the afternoon Mrs Page missed a bonnet. Mrs Page informed the police, and PC Evans went to Bedford in search of the prisoner, where he met her in the street wearing the stolen bonnet. She confessed to stealing the bonnet, but said she had picked the sovereign up off the floor. It appeared the prisoner had previously been convicted and undergone a sentence at a reformatory. At Rutland Lent Assizes she pleaded guilty and was sentenced to six months hard labour.

An extraordinary case of theft was brought against a navvy woman from the Railway Huts at Gretton. Isabella King, 33, a dressmaker, was charged with stealing five beds, 12 blankets, 12 sheets, five counterpanes, a boiler, three saucepans, a kettle, and a quantity of woollen shirts, together valued at £20, and all the property of Josiah Moore, the man she was living with. She was sentenced to two months hard labour.

Another dressmaker, Elizabeth Wells, 24, was charged with stealing a money box, six gold and three jet studs, and £9 16s from No 13 Hut, Glaston, the property of James Holder. Superintendent Murfitt traced her to London, and apprehended her, after she had absconded. She was found guilty, and the penalty was six weeks hard labour.

The rape of Mrs Smith

'A true bill was returned against James Simmons (22), labourer, and John Jennings (22) for committing a rape upon Roseanne Smith, at Seaton, on 22nd November, and at the same place stealing from her person certain monies. Both prisoners pleaded not guilty. Mr

Lawrence, QC and Mr Buzzard, QC conducted the case for the prosecution, and Mr Bennett, QC defended the prisoners. The complainant, Mrs Roseanne Smith, is the wife of Thomas Smith, navvy, employed on the railway now being constructed between Manton and Kettering. On 22nd November, Mrs Smith went from Manton to Seaton to see her husband, and stayed at The Three Horseshoes public house until closing time, when she left intoxicated, accompanied by three men, two of whom were the prisoners and another named Pincher, not in custody. They conducted her down a lane on pretence of escorting her to the huts, where her husband lodged, and there committed the offence. The witnesses, seven in number, were subjected to a severe cross-examination. The jury were addressed at length by councils on both sides. The jury, after retiring for ½ hour, returned a verdict of guilty against both prisoners, accompanied by a recommendation of mercy on account of their youth. His Lordship, Sir Nathaniel Lindley, Knight, said he regretted to see the prisoners in such a sorry condition, but could not help but feeling that the verdict was entirely right, and although they had recommended the prisoners to mercy, it was important to remember that although a woman was intoxicated, it was no reason why she should be violated. He could not treat the matter lightly, and should be failing in his duty if he did, and he therefore sentenced each of the accused to five years penal servitude. This case lasted five hours.'

On 1 April a newspaper report told of the removal of the convicts from Oakham Gaol to Pentonville Penal Prison.

Manslaughter at the tunnel

'Alleged manslaughter at Corby: On the 21st inst George Hibbs, a ganger, employed on the Kettering to Manton Railway, and stationed at Corby Huts, was apprehended on suspicion of causing the death of his wife on the preceding night. An inquest was heard on the 23rd, and from the evidence it appeared that the accused and his wife had been drinking at a hut on the Gretton side of Corby Tunnel, and on their way back to Corby a quarrel ensued, when Hibbs so injured his wife that she died during the night. Mr Greaves, surgeon, of Weldon, said deceased's face, hands and arms were very much bruised. There were some clots of extravasated blood on the brain, quite sufficient to cause death. The jury, after consulting for an hour, returned a verdict of manslaughter, and Hibbs was committed for trial.'

As reported by the *Stamford Mercury* on 31 January 1879, those were the facts brought before the inquest at Corby on the body of Harriett Hibbs. Gretton Tunnel, or Corby Tunnel, runs beneath part of the parishes of Gretton and Corby. At that time it was being worked down ten shafts, and the various sections came under sub-contractors, foremen and gangers. George Hibbs was one of those. We know of the large hut settlement at Corby Wood, where, at No 19, lived Hibbs with his wife, Harriett Elizabeth, and at least two children, Anne Elizabeth, 13 years old, and her brother, whose age and name I do not know. At No 1, Gretton Huts, lived a labourer called Jones, with his wife, Mary, and their 14-year-old son, William. It would seem that this was one of the huts where drink was sold. One of their neighbours was Elizabeth Rowe. At No 19 lived a labourer called Thomas Lines, and at another hut nearby lived a timekeeper called Henry Linger. This group of huts was part of a settlement on the top of the tunnel at the Gretton end. All these people, including the older children, gave evidence at the inquest, and from this and the trial of George Hibbs I have construed the story.

In evidence, Mary Jones stated that Mrs Hibbs had gone to her hut about 4 o'clock, and soon afterwards Hibbs came in with a man called Linger. Mrs Hibbs had two or three little drinks of gin, and her husband and Linger had three or four pints of beer. About

7.30 Mrs Hibbs wanted to go home, but Hibbs was not ready to go. Neither Hibbs nor his wife seemed to be drunk. At Mrs Hibbs's request Mary Jones and William went with her. Mary turned back, having told William to accompany Mrs Hibbs the rest of the way. As she was returning she met Hibbs, and said that William was taking his wife home, and he would soon catch them up.

William then took up the account. After verifying his mother's evidence, he said that as they reached No 7 Shaft, Hibbs came running up behind them, and made as if to strike them. William was frightened and ran away. In answer to questions he said he had not heard blows struck, but did hear Mrs Hibbs cry out several times. Henry Linger, the timekeeper who had been drinking with Hibbs, said that Hibbs and his wife were on friendly terms at Jones's hut, and neither were drunk. Elizabeth Rowe, in evidence, said that she had heard a woman's screams coming from the direction of No 7 Shaft, and a man say, 'Get up.' Thomas Lines said that he had seen Mrs Hibbs going towards her hut with the boy William Jones. He went to Jones's hut, and saw Hibbs there, who left soon afterwards. Neither Mrs Hibbs nor her husband were drunk when he saw them. Lines went home, and soon afterwards he heard screams from the direction of No 7 Shaft, but did not hear a man. The next morning he went with Police Sergeant Meadows, and they found blood and signs of a struggle.

The Hibbs's 13-year-old daughter, Anne Elizabeth, said that as her father and mother had not come home by about a quarter to ten, she and her little brother went to look for them. When they got to the shaft, they found their mother lying on the ground and their father trying to get her up. Between them they got her home, and Anne put her to bed. About 4 in the morning Hibbs woke her, saying, 'Oh Annie, I believe your mother is dead.' He then went to Seaton to fetch her grandmother. On being questioned Anne said that her parents were not in the habit of quarrelling. Police Sergeant Meadows gave evidence of blood and other signs of a severe struggle near the shaft. Hibbs was taken into custody by Inspector Barwell. Dr Greaves, of Weldon, gave evidence of the injuries he found on examining the body, and what he found during his post-mortem examination. He said that no sharp instrument had been used. Death may have been caused by apoplexy or a fall or a heavy blow with a fist.

The jury returned a verdict of manslaughter, and Hibbs was committed for trial. On 30 January he was taken before a Special Petty Sessional Court. By then the charge had been amended to wilful murder. Similar evidence was given at that hearing as at the inquest, though more details came to light, including the fact that Mrs Hibbs was an epileptic, and when she suffered the fits, she would fight and scream violently. Hibbs was represented by Mr English, a solicitor from Stamford, who moved that there was no evidence to substantiate the capital charge of wilful murder, and asked that he be put on trial for manslaughter. This plea had no effect, and Hibbs was brought before Sir Robert Lush at the Spring Assizes at Northampton on 23 April. Again there was additional evidence. It appeared that Mrs Hibbs had wanted to go home in a Mr Brown's cart, but Hibbs would not let her. It also appeared that both Hibbs and his wife were indeed drunk. Evidence was also given by George Hibbs's mother, whom it will be remembered was fetched from Seaton. Police and medical evidence was given as before, but in more detail. There were two other doctors present – Dr Bayley of Duston and Dr Duke from Great Easton – in whose opinion the blood clot on the brain found at the post-mortem might have been caused by a fall or a blow.

In the light of that, the Judge said that the evidence bore out the fact that the deceased might have met with her death through injuries she received through falling down, and the prosecution had failed to substantiate the charge of wilful murder. At this, Mr Jacques, who led the prosecution, withdrew. The Jury retired for a short time, then the Foreman gave their opinion that the evidence had failed to show the deceased had met her death at the hands of the prisoner. The Judge concurred with the verdict, and Hibbs was discharged.

Harriett was buried at Corby on 26 January

Names from police and court reports

Many of the following have appeared in the text.

Allen, Joseph: Rushton
Althorpe, Joseph alias Flinkey: Kettering
Anderson, George: Chipping Norton
Applegate, John: Wiltshire
Arnold, Aaron: Glaston
Atkins, Fred: Seaton
Ball, Henry: Rothwell
Banks, Charles: Stanton
Bennett, William: Seaton
Bodlington: Braunston
Bradley, Alfred: Seaton
Braunston, James alias Brumagem: Seaton
Brookes, John alias Nottingham Jack: Seaton
Brown, Charles: Coventry
Brown, John: Glaston
Burcher, William: Rushton
Cheshire, William: Glaston
Clarke, Henry: Seaton
Clarke, Arthur William: Caldecott
Clarke, John: Walsall
Coleman, William: Seaton
Cooper: Rushton
Cue, William: Whittlesea
Cunnington, William: Seaton
Daniels, Eliza: Wing
Davies, John: Seaton
Dickenson, John: Grantham
Downs
Durrant
Edis, William: Seaton
Edwards, David: Glaston
Edwards, George: Corby
Evans, Edward: Worcester
Fardint, Cardine: Wing
Goff, Samuel: Corby
Goiner, John: Seaton
Gowers, John alias Cockney: Glaston
Green, John: Westminster
Hamm, William

Hardy, William: Seaton
Harris, Henry: Gretton
Harris, Josiah: Buckinghamshire
Harrison, George: Seaton
Harvey, Frederick: Leicester
Hawes, William: Corby
Haydon, Samuel
Hibbs, George: Corby
Holdman, Enoch: Corby
Hopkins: Portsmouth
Hunter, James William: Salford
Jennings, John: Seaton
Jesson, William: Barrowden
Johnson, Thomas: Kettering
Jones, John: Wiltshire
King, Isabella: Gretton
Law, John: Rushton
Lee, George: Leicester
Liance, John: Kettering
Lowe, Henry: Gretton
Lusted
Mattson, Henry: Glaston
March, Charles: Glaston
Marlow, Robert: Rushton
Martin, William
Meredith, John: South Wales
Mills, Robert: North America
Mitchell
Moore, John alias Allen: Glaston
Morton, Benjamin: Seaton
Munns, Stephen: Earith
Newton, William
Noel, George
Pearson, Charles: Seaton
Phillips, Joseph
Proctor, Richard: Redditch
Read, Walter or Wallace: Glaston
Rivvett, Samuel: Glendon
Robinson: Seaton
Sawday, Edward
Shaw, John: Glaston

Shelborne, Thomas
Simmons, James: Seaton
Small, John
Smith, John: Seaton
Smith, Harry: Bristol
Smith, William
Spake: Wing
Spreadborough, William alias King: Seaton
Stafford, John alias Allen
Stanger, George: Gretton
Stones: Wing
Swift, James: Glaston
Taylor, John
Taylor, Joseph: Morcott
Taylor, Josiah
Throsby, C.: Corby
Thorn, William
Turner, William: Essex
Ward, John: Glendon
Warner, Charles
Wells, Elizabeth: Glaston
'Welsh Jimmy': Glaston
White, John alias Ginger: Seaton
White, John: Seaton
White, Samuel
White, William
Williams, John alias Soldier: Seaton
Williams, John: Dover
Williams, John: Rushton
Williams, George: Finchley
Williams, Henry
Williamson, George
Wills, James
Wilson, Alfred: Barrowden
Wilson, William
Withell, Mary Anne: Seaton
Wollett: Chipping Norton
Wright, Joseph: Glaston
Wyman, Geo.: Seaton
Yates, Henry

1879, and a note in the margin of the Burial Register reads: 'Died it is supposed by her husband's hand.' She was 32.

There were contemporary conflicting views on the amount of criminal behaviour brought into the district by the railway. For example, in March 1878, under Police reports in the county of Rutland, we find: 'The number of offences in this county is kept up by the great number of workmen employed on the railway works in the course of construction. There has been a slight increase in vagrancy.' And yet in the same week, at the Rutland Assizes, Baron Cleasby congratulated the Jury on the freedom from crime. Mr Henry Frewen, also in March 1878, remarked that when he qualified for a magistrate for the county of Rutland about 42 years ago, the average number of prisoners in the gaol was from 20 to 25. Now there were only two under sentence and none for trial. He attributed the decrease to the very rigid discipline enforced in the Oakham Prison, which, he considered, had a very salutary effect. Once a person got a taste of the punishment in Rutland Gaol they never wanted to go there any more. He said a year in Oakham was quite equal to two in any other gaol.

In this chapter some of the crimes committed by the navvies have been highlighted, but there were many more that I have not recorded. Yet I still maintain that compared with the vast numbers of railway people who lived and toiled along the whole length of the line, crimes were relatively few. Most of them fell into the familiar categories of poaching, drunken behaviour, sleeping rough, and minor theft, crimes traditionally associated with navvy life and which were dealt with most severely. There were, I agree, other more extreme cases. But these, in any community and any walk of life, would be considered most serious.

12
RAILWAY FAMILIES FROM THE REGISTERS

At the beginning of this book I said that little had been written about the railway navvies, and that a hundred years or so later the majority are as anonymous as those who built the pyramids. One of my aims was to redress this. Many have indeed now emerged from the past, albeit briefly, as people with real lives and families, and their names have appeared in preceding chapters. It has been suggested to me that genealogists would be interested if I included all the names I could find, even if the people concerned have not featured as individual personalities in the text. So once again I set out on several trawling expeditions to gather what I could from more parish registers. These registers give a very clear insight into the numbers of trades and skills involved in the building of a railway. Some clergy had more of an eye for the future than others, and included interesting comments. To them, over a century later, I am truly grateful.

Abbreviations

A	accountant	FF	foreman fitter	RHK	railway horsekeeper
B	banksman	FL	farm labourer	RL	railway labourer
BL	bricklayer	G	ganger	RSI	railway signal
BM	brickmaker	GK	gatekeeper		inspector
BB	brickburner	L	labourer	RW	railway worker
C	carpenter	M	miner	s	son
Con	contractor	Mc	mechanic	S	sawyer
d	daughter	PL	platelayer	SCon	subcontractor
ED	engine driver	RB	railway blacksmith	SM	shoemaker
En	engineer	RC	railway clerk	T	turner
EF	engine fitter	RE	railway engineer	TK	time keeper
Ex	excavator	RF	railway foreman	Tr	tailor
F	fitter				

Railway families appearing in Glaston Baptism Register

All of these families were given as living in the railway huts at Glaston, with the exception of Henry and Hannah Weight, who were recorded as living at the Wing Railway Huts.

BAKER, Richard and Elizabeth   M
    d   Susan
    s   Richard William
BUDDEN, Harris and Mary Jane   SCon
    s   Charles Henry
    d   Alice Mary
    s   George Robert
    s   William Horace

s	Frederick John	
s	Henry Francis	
CANNOCK, George and Elizabeth		RB
s	Alfred	
d	Elizabeth	
COOPER, William and Sarah		RF
s	Herbert	
COOPER, Benjamin and Emma		M
s	Frederick	
COOPER, Thomas and Agnes		M
d	Annie	
COUSINS, John and Catherine		C
s	George Edward	
s	Alga Frank	
CREASEY, John and Caroline		RL
d	Annie Sarah Maria	
d	Caroline Louisa	
s	Alfred Thomas	
CURTIS, William and Elizabeth,		TK
d	Elizabeth Woolston	
DAVIS, William and Janette Amelia		ED
d	Rose Anne Maria	
DEERING, Samuel and Rachel Maria		C
s	William Frederick	
s	Henry Frederick	
d	Alice Maud Dolly	
DOUGLAS, William and Isabella		F
d	Francis Anne Lambert	
FINCH, William Henry and Jane		SCon
s	Harry	
GODLEY, Tom and Olivia Julia		RL
d	Sarah Elizabeth	
d	Frances	
GOULD, Samuel and Mary Anne		PL
s	Samuel Oliver	
HILLMAN,		
Hugh Richard and Emily Anne		ED
s	Thomas Obadiah	
s	George Henry	
s	William Hugh	
d	Clara Elizabeth	
HOLDER, James and Anne		M
s	John	
HINDLETON, Richard and Esther		M
d	Maria	
JEFFREY, Samuel and Harriett		ED
d	Nelly	
d	Edith Anne	
d	Jessie	
KNIGHT, Thomas and Harriett		M
d	Ada	

KNIGHT, William and Sarah		Con
s	Henry	
KNIGHT, George and Ellen		RL
s	George Henry	
MARCH, Charles and Jemima		S
s	Charles	
MEES, Martha (single mother)		
d	Temperance	
MILLWOOD,		
Jonathan Jones and Harriett		BM
s	Jonathan Thomas	
NICHOLLS, Henry and Ellen		ED
d	Hannah	
OLIVER, John George and Mary Isabella		M
s	Robert George	
PAYNE, Thomas and Mary		B
s	Thomas	
PLOWMAN, Henry and Clara		SCon
s	Herbert Samuel	
STEVENS, Robert James and		RHK
	Olive Ann	
d	Mary Anne	
TAYLOR, Henry and Elizabeth		RW
d	Mary Anne	
THOMAS, Richard and Charlotte		M
d	Laura	
WAKEFIELD, Joseph and Alice		BM
s	Joseph Charles	
WEIGHT, Henry and Hannah		ED
d	Maria Maude	
WEIGHT, Frederick Henry and Maria		ED
s	Frederick Henry	
WILLS,		
Charles Joseph and Frances Amelia		RE
d	Frances Amelia	
d	Ada Beatrice	
WILLIAMS, John and Eleanor		RL
d (twin)	Louisa	
d (twin)	Eleanor	
WITCHAM, John and Mary		RW
d	Ada	

The Budden family are interesting, in that they were all baptised on the same day, 4 January 1880. Their birth years were noted as 1866, 1868, 1871, 1873, 1874 and 1876. Elizabeth Cannock died four months after her baptism. William and Henry Deering, both, interestingly enough, with Frederick as their second name, were baptised on the same day, 3 June 1877, aged four and two. Their sister was baptised three months later. Thomas Obadiah Hillman died 18 days after his baptism. Susan Baker also died within months. The Williams twins were born and baptised in March 1878, and both were buried on 10 February 1879. The three Creasey children were all baptised on 21 April 1876, Caroline was five and Alfred two and a half; presumably Annie was an infant. Rev Barnard Smith conducted four of the baptisms, Rev D. W. Barrett 36, Rev Christopher Wordsworth 20, and Rev J. H. Skrine, of Uppingham School, one (Skrine was the author of *Uppingham-by-the-Sea*, mentioned in Chapter 10).

Glaston burials of railway people from the Register

23 Mar 1877	John Jones Roberts
17 May 1877	Daniel Giblin (?), 60
24 June 1877	John Stone, 34
16 Aug 1877	John Pickwick
8 Aug 1877	Elizabeth Cannock, 6 months

There are many unmarked navvy graves in Glaston churchyard, but beside the path, much weathered and so difficult to make out, is the headstone of Daniel Juett, aged 78. Barrett, in his introductory note, mentions several men whom we have met among our '3000 Strangers', and D. Juett is among them. Typically Barrett did not divulge the reason for his mention. *Ted Reynolds*

28 Aug 1877	Henry Yates alias George Clarke, 35
27 Nov 1877	Charles Brackenbury, 27
25 Dec 1877	Henry Knight, 3 months
29 Jan 1878	Thomas Wilcock, 6 months
4 Mar 1878	John Holder, 10 weeks
9 Mar 1879	Daniel Juett, 78

These were all living in the railway huts. We met John Stone, John Pickwick and Charles Brackenbury in Chapter 10. Daniel Juett is interesting, for beside his name is the comment 'formerly a miner on the first Thames Tunnel'. He has an elaborate gravestone, now much weathered. Of the many railway graves in the churchyards along the line, Daniel Juett and Thomas Winfield at Great Oakley (see Chapter 4) are the only two I have found commemorated with a gravestone.

Glaston marriages of railway people from the Register

Unless otherwise indicated by 'W', the brides and grooms were spinsters and bachelors. GRH indicates Glaston Railway Huts; the hut number was sometimes recorded. SL indicates South Luffenham.

1876
16 Oct: ASHLEY, William John (RL) and Elizabeth Anne LIDINGTON (16)
No fathers recorded: both born before marriage
Witnesses Philip and Mary THORN

25 Dec: WELLS, Henry Albert (C), GRH, and Sarah SEWELL, GRH
Fathers Thomas WELLS (C) and Francis SEWELL (FL)
Witnesses Thomas Alfred and Elizabeth WELLS

1877
10 Mar: RUSSELL, James (M), GRH, and Emily JENNER, GRH
Fathers George RUSSELL (FL) and David JENNER (SM)
Witnesses Richard and Emily BRACH

22 Oct: CHANDLER, Frederick (M) and
 Frances Elizabeth SWANN (both GRH)
Fathers James CHANDLER (C) and John
 SWANN (L)
Witnesses Mary Frances SWANN and
 Thomas LEWIS

25 Dec: NASH Samuel (M), GRH, and
 Sarah Anne WILLIAMS (W), GRH
Fathers William NASH (L) and James
 HOLDER (BL)
Witnesses Charlotte THOMAS and G.
 KING

1878
9 Apr: FULLER, Frederic (M), No 26 GRH,
 and Mary Jane BAKER (W), GRH
Fathers James FULLER (L) and James
 LAMBERT (M)
Witnesses James LESTER and Caroline
 BARNETT

22 Apr: WAKEFIELD, Joseph (brickyard L),
 No 28 GRH, and Alice HILL, No 27
 GRH
Fathers George WAKEFIELD (L) and
 Charles HILL (L)
Witnesses Alfred and Sarah Anne
 HELLMAN

1879
12 Jun: HUDSON, William (L), SL, and
 Elizabeth Anne LATTIMER, GRH
Fathers Samuel HUDSON (RL) and Henry
 LATTIMER (L)
Witnesses John HUDSON and Sarah Jane
 LATTIMER

I have included the Hudson marriage because
as William's father was a labourer on the
railway, it is probable that William was also. In
addition to the Railway Mission, Barrett was in
charge of Glaston parish between the death of
Rev Barnard Smith and the arrival of Rev
Christopher Wordsworth as incumbent. I had
vaguely wondered why in 1878 Barrett had
started to sign himself 'Curate in Charge', so I
am grateful to Rutland Historical and Record
Society for the information that between April
and November 1878 Christopher Wordsworth
went to Cornwall to take temporary charge of

St Mary's, Truro, and Glaston parish was thus
once again in Barrett's care.

Railway families appearing in Seaton Baptism Register

It will be remembered that there were 35 huts
occupied at Seaton by the navvies working for
Lucas & Aird, and 10 occupied by those
employed by Messrs Moss, the contractors for
the LNWR line from Seaton to Wansford. It
would appear that Barrett had an input into
their welfare too, as he baptised several of
their children and buried several of their dead.
I have indicated with an asterisk (*) the
LNWR families if it was noted in the register.

ACKLAND,
 Thomas Warwick and Charlotte   RC
  d   Amy Louise
ALBON, Isaac and Ellen   RL*
  s   Edwin
  d   Ellen
  d   Annie
AMOS, ? and Lucy   BM
  s   John
BACON, James Alexander and
 Elizabeth Anne   C, TK
  s   John William
BAXTER, Samuel and Elizabeth   RL*
  d   Alice Emma
BOTTING, John and Mary Jane   ED
  s   Ernest Edward
BOWLDEN, James and Mary Ann   BM
  s   Ernest Walter
BROUGHAM, Fred and Fanny   En
  d   Lauretta
CLARKE, Elizabeth (spinster)
  s   Charles Edwin Neal
COUSINS, Arthur and Mary Jane   PL
  s   Frederick
CURTIS, William and Elizabeth   T
  d   Frances Elizabeth
DAILOW, Samuel and Mary Anne   RB
  d   Kate Anne
DICKENS, George and Mary   BM
  d   Rose Anne
EVANS, Edward and Harriet   BM
  d   Isabella
FALL, Joseph and Mary   RHK*
  d   Elizabeth

FORBES, John and Sarah		F
s	Malcolm Matthew	
GAMBRIEL, George and Sarah Anne		RL*
d	Ellen	
GARDINER, George William and Emily		RL
s	Ernest George	
GARDINER, George Wallace and June		BM
d	Edith Emma	
GREY, William and Sarah		F
s	William	
GREEN, William and Mary		RL
d	Elizabeth Esther	
HAWKSWELL, Samuel and Emma		BM
d	Elizabeth	
HERCOCK, William and Jane Emily		T
s	James Herbert	
HOLLINE?,		
	Louis Urban Peveril and Susan Jane	G
s	Louis Urban Peveril	
HOOKER, John and Mary		BM
d	Hannah Elizabeth	
HOPCROFT, John and Mary		Tr*
s	John Robert	
Adult baptism, aged 29, private		
HOSKINS, Louisa		
s	George	
JENKINS,		
	George Job and Sarah Creedy Hall	ED
s	Job Henry	
JONES, John and Augusta		BL
s	John	
LORDEN, William Henry and Melina		SCon
s	John	
MIDDLETON, George and Elizabeth		BM
d	Emily Rose Hannah	
MILES, Henry and Louisa		ED
d	Emma Elizabeth	
d	Frances Ellen	
d	Mary Anne	
PARKER, Thomas and Mary		C
s	John Thomas	
PICKERING, William and Mary Jane		RSI
d	Gertrude	
s	Edmund	
d	Catherine	
READ, William & Emma		PL
s	George	
REEVE, Frederick and Hannah		M
s	Luke Charity	
ROGERS, Charles and Hannah		RB*
d	Georgina	

SHELDON, Charles Henry and Annie		F
s	Edwin Henry	
d	Emma Jane	
SHELDON, Horace Henry and Julia		T
s	William Charles Edward	
d	Lillian Alice	
SILLIAH(?), Edward and Elizabeth		BL
s	Francis	
SIMMONS, William and Ellen		RL
s	Robert William	
SMITH, Thomas and Sarah Anne		Ex
d	Lucy Francis	
STOKES, William John and Jane		ED
d	Annie	
d	Sarah Jane	
TANSLEY, John and Mary Ann		ED
s	Thomas Henry	
s	Thomas Edward	
TOMBLIN, James Pridmore and Ruth		PL
s	Alfred Pridmore	
TOMLINSON, William and Anne		RB
d	Edith Maria	
WARBURTON,		
	Edmund Ashcroft and Betty Anne	RB
d	Edith Gertrude	
WEBSTER, George and Ada		RL
s	Alfred	
d	Annie Elizabeth	
WELSH-MOSS, John and Mary Ann		BM
d	Phoebe Amy	
d	Mary Ann Emily	
d	Clara	
WOOD, William and Sarah		F
s	George William	
d	Ada Anne	

Mr Pickering, the railway signal inspector, appears twice, on 30 July 1876 and 27 July 1879. His address was given as Foxhole, near Swansea, Glamorganshire. John Lorden was the 15-year-old son of the subcontractor for the Welland Viaduct. Mr Warburton the blacksmith had Cheadle, Cheshire, noted by his name, and Mr Cousins the platelayer had Kilsby in his entry.

Occasionally the hut number was recorded: the Gardiner family lived at No 20 Midland Railway Huts, Green at No 4, Miles at No 3, Bowlden at No 41, Hercock at No 27. The Fall family was at No 6 LNWR huts.

Seaton burials of railway people from the Register

From this Register I have included the addresses as given, as well as dates and ages. I have also included the initials of Rev D. W. Barrett and Rev Thomas Heycock, the incumbent at Seaton, for they indicate how balanced the duties were between them.

31 Jan 1876	Ernest George Gardiner (2 days), 22 Railway Huts TH
9 Oct 1876	Joseph Bedford (42), 5 Railway Huts TH
19 Oct 1876	Charles Enden (18), 15 Railway Huts DWB
17 Dec 1876	William Morton (34), Midland Railway Works TH
20 Dec 1876	John Thomas Manton (24), Midland Railway Works TH
22 Dec 1876	Henry Gill (46), Seaton Huts DWB
18 Feb 1877	John Short (70), Seaton Huts DWB
25 Apr 1877	Alice Jenkins (1 month), Seaton Railway Huts TH
30 Apr 1877	Alfred Clarke (26) TH
4 May 1877	Elizabeth Louise Bennett (21), Midland Railway Works DWB
21 Sep 1877	John Robert Hopcroft (29), Seaton LNWR DWB
3 Jan 1878	Mary Anne Welch (33), Midland Railway Huts TH
7 Jan 1878	John Williams (23), Seaton LNWR Huts TH
14 Feb 1878	William Banks (67), Midland Railway Huts TH
24 Mar 1878	Thomas Henry Tansley (5 months), Seaton Railway Huts TH
7 Apr 1878	James Duggen (60), Seaton Railway Huts TH
7 Apr 1878	Ernest William Oxenham (11 months), Seaton Railway Canteen TH
19 May 1879	Willie Chapman (1 year 8 months), Seaton Railway Huts, James V. Crispin, Officiating Minister
5 Feb 1880	Ann Dixon (77), Midland Railway Huts TH

By the time little Willie Chapman had died, Barrett had moved on, as we will see in Chapter 13. Probably Rev Thomas Heycock was away, so Rev J. V. Crispin, the incumbent at Harringworth, conducted the funeral. William Morton was, according to the Register, lodging in the village. John Thomas Manton was also living in the village. Alfred Clarke's fatal accident was related in Chapter 6. Rev Thomas Heycock made an additional note by the entry in the Burial Register: '(Registered Alfred Clarke SMITH), 26 years. Accidentally killed on Midland Railway Works in Tunnel near Coach Bridge.' It may be remembered that in the section on the tunnels in Chapter 6 the accidental death of Frederick Clarke Smith was recalled from the newspaper report. It seems to me that there was either an error in the press or, less likely, the Register, for this must surely be the same fatality. Elizabeth Louise Bennett is rather puzzling, for though she was lodging in the village, she was registered Midland Railway Works. I wonder whether she helped out at the 'shant'. John Hopcroft was baptised as an adult shortly before his death. Mary Anne Welch is Mary Anne Welch-Moss, whose story appears in Chapter 6. James Duggen died at the Uppingham Union.

Seaton marriages of railway people from the Register

Unless otherwise stated by 'W', the brides and grooms were spinsters and bachelors. Rev Thomas Heycock conducted all these marriages. The occupation abbreviations are as before (see page 120).

1876
7 Jun: ELSTON, John (RL) and Eliza FURNESS (W), both Seaton
Fathers Matthew ELSTON and Joseph CANNON (both RL)
Witnesses Elisha and Eliza STOPHARD

18 Jun: MURPHY, Dennis (RL) and Margaret POWELL (W), both Seaton
Fathers Daniel MURPHY and Daniel HEIRON (both RL)
Witnesses William MURPHY and Lucy ANSTEL

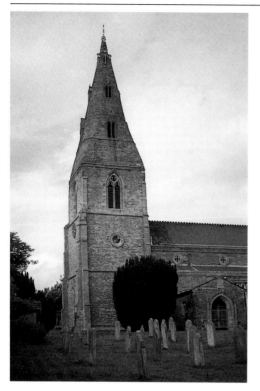

Seaton church. Mary Anne Welsh-Moss is buried in the churchyard in an unmarked grave, as are many other railway people. *Author*

26 Aug: EVANS, Edward (W) (BM), 22 MR Huts, and Harriett ATKINS, Thorpe by Water
Fathers Edward EVANS (BM) and William Atkins (GK)
Witnesses W. ATKINS and Betsy Anne ATKINS

3 Sep: FORBES John (W) (Mc) and Sarah MUNTON
No details provided

1877
15 Jan: SMITH, Thomas (Ex) and Sarah Anne CUNNINGTON (both Seaton)
Fathers John SMITH (Ex) and David CUNNINGTON (RL)
I omitted to note the witnesses

5 Feb: FRISBY, Henry (RL), Wing, and Elizabeth ORTON (Seaton)

Fathers William FRISBY and John ORTON (both RL)
Witnesses William MEADSWELL and Mary Anne FRISBY

19 May: HOLLINGSWORTH, George Edward (BM) and Mary Jane CLARKE (both Seaton Railway Huts)
Fathers George HOLLINGSWORTH (BM) and James CLARKE (BL)
Witnesses Frederick and Betsy Anne ATKINS

21 May: OAKLAND, George (BM) and Louisa WARD (both Seaton)
Fathers Henry OAKLAND (BM) and Thomas WARD (RL)
Witnesses Thomas and Emma TRIGG

2 Sep: WELSH, John (BB) and Mary Anne MOSS (W), both 20, MR Huts
Fathers George WELSH (BM) and James FLETCHER (RL)
Witnesses John FOSTER and Mary Ann SMITHERSMAN

13 Sep: HODDER, Henry M. and Clara ANDREWS (W), both Seaton
Fathers Joshua HODDER (road controller) and Daniel BOARD (assistant relieving officer)
Witnesses George and Ada WEBSTER

1878
1 Jan: SIMMONS William M. and Ella SMITH, both Seaton
Fathers Elias SIMMONS (farm bailiff) and Thomas SMITH (RL)
Witnesses George and Kate SMITH

12 Jan: HIBBS, Walter (RL) and Elizabeth CLACK, both Seaton
Fathers Isaac HIBBS (foreman excavator) and James CLACK (or CLARKE) (RL)
Witnesses Frederick STANGER and Ann(?) BROWN

12 Jan: ATKINS, Frederick (RL) and Clara GOODLIFFE, both Seaton
Fathers William ATKINS (GK) and William GOODLIFFE (RL)

Witnesses Frederick STANGER and Ann(?) BROWN

4 Feb: DUNBOVIN(?), George (ED) and Louisa HOSKINS, both Seaton
Fathers George DUNBOVIN(?) (ED) and George HOSKINS (S)
Witnesses William ATMORE and Fanny JONES

12 Mar: CUNNINGTON, Charles Henry (RL) and Margaret Ann ALBON, both Seaton
Fathers David CUNNINGTON (L) and John ALBON (L)
Witnesses Thomas and Sarah Ann SMITH

15 Oct: BROWETT, Frederick (railway porter), Thorpe by Water, and Eliza WEBSTER, Uppingham
Fathers Charles BROWETT (L) and George WEBSTER (L)
Witnesses George WEBSTER and Emma WEBSTER

8 Jul: PATTINSON, George (RL) and Elizabeth VIRGIN, 27 MR Huts
Fathers George PATTINSON and James VIRGIN (both RL)
Witnesses James and Sarah BANKS

From the surnames in the Murphy wedding, I have concluded that they may be Irish.

Railway families appearing in Harringworth Baptism Register

Some of the labourers may not have been on the railway – Rev J. V. Crispin was not very informative.

COOKE, Robert Stephen and Elizabeth		A
s	Edmund Robert	
DAMS, Henry and Sarah		L
d	Lily Jane Mary	
DOWNS(?), Thomas and Amelia Anne		ED
d	Amelia	
GUNNEL, Edward and Charlotte		L
d	Elizabeth Emma	
HACKETT, George and Eliza		L
d	Ellen Gertrude	

OXENHAM, Thomas Henry and Sarah		
	shopkeeper/canteen proprietor	
d	Caroline	
s	Ernest William	
SMITH, Alfred and Anne		L
d	Ada	
SMITH, William and Naomi Jane		L
d	Roseanne	
SMITH, William and Sarah Anne		L
s	William	
s	John Richard	
STAPLETON, John and Martha		L
d	Anne	
STAPLETON, Henry William and Emma		
	policeman	
s	Henry William	
d	Emily	
d	Sarah	
THORPE, Edward and Catherine		L
s	Herbert	
s	George	
THORNE, Joseph and Anne Elizabeth		
Station Master		
s	Joseph	
WARD, Thomas and Margaret		L
s	George Henry	
WYMAN, David and Mary Anne		L
s	Joseph	

All of these baptisms were conducted by Rev James V. Crispin. Mr Ward had Wakefield, Yorkshire, by his entry in the Register. PC Stapleton had Hinckley by his name, but I have not found him involved in any cases. Mr Cooke, the accountant, was in the Midland Railway Company's office, according to the Register, and his address was given as Arboretum Street, Derby. Joseph, Station Master Thorne's son, was baptised in 1880.

There were no obvious railway people in the Harringworth marriage or burial registers.

Railway families appearing in Gretton Baptism Register

It will be noticed that the majority of these fathers were employed either as miners, that is to say were driving the tunnel through, or labourers. Most of these families lived in

Gretton Huts, while the Knowles, Proctor and Bloomfield families were at Crestwell or Cresswell Huts. Several lived in the village itself, presumably in lodgings, since they were not local. For the remainder, there was nothing in the Register to indicate where they lived.

BLABER, John and Elizabeth   RL
   d   Mary Elizabeth
BLOOMFIELD, Arthur and Caroline   RL
   d   Anne Elizabeth
CLARKE, Samuel Joseph and Annie   mason
   d   Florence Isabella
COX, William and Elizabeth   M
   s   Robert
CROW, George and Lizzie   RL
   d   Margaret Hannah
HARDING, Samuel and Ellen   M
   d   Fanny
HUBBARD, Isaac and Augusta   BM
   d   Emma Mary
JINKS, John and Mary Ann   RL
   s   Robert William
JOHNSON, Thomas and Eliza   drainer
   s   Albert
KIMPLOW, William and Sarah Jane   RL
   d   Harriet
KNOWLES, Henry and Martha   RL
   s   Cornelius
   s   Henry William
LAWRENCE, Thomas and Martha   RL
   d   Violet Ellen
LAWRENCE, William and Maria   RL
   d   Mary Maud
LEATHERLAND, Sam and Sarah   BL
   d   Susannah
MARTINDALE, Luke and Sarah   RL
   s   Robert
PETCH, Charles and Bessie   BL
   d   Kate Grace
PROCTOR, Joseph and Mary Ann   RL
   s   George Henry
PULLEN, Robert and Mary   stonemason
   s   Robert
REDWAY(?), James and Elizabeth   RL
   s   John James
SILVERTON, Edward and Elizabeth   BL
   d   Emily Maud
TALBOT, John and Alice Elizabeth   M
   s   George

WOOLSEY, John & Lydia   RL
   s   Henry
   s   Thomas William

Gretton burials of railway people from the Register

21 May 1876   Thomas West (30)
4 Jun 1876   George Joseph Talbot (4)
17 Jun 1876   William Caseley (36)
18 Dec 1876   Edward Harwood (37)
6 Mar 1877   Sarah Ann Bloomfield (4)
2 Apr 1877   Emily Rosanna Middleton
            (6 weeks)
15 Jun 1877   Elizabeth Mayers Archer (50)
10 Jul 1877   Ellen Harding (42)
2 Sep 1877   William Knight (45)
15 Oct 1877   Samuel Smith and
            Thomas Jones
20 Oct 1878   William Wyman (14)

George Joseph Talbot was a ganger's son. The Middleton family and William Knight lived at Gretton Huts. The Bloomfield and Harding families lived at Crestwell Huts, as did Elizabeth Archer. The tragedy of Sarah Ann Bloomfield was related in Chapter 10. Ellen Harding was buried a month after the baptism of her daughter Fanny. Samuel Smith and Thomas Jones were the two men found dead in a ditch, as related in Chapter 10. William Wyman was killed at the railway tip; he was of a local family but I speculate he may have been employed as a tip boy on the long embankment.

Gretton marriages of railway people from the Register

1876
21 Nov: ROODAWAY, John (M) and Annie Elizabeth WALKER, both Gretton Huts

30 Dec: SHONE, John (M) and Mary Anne TOOMBS, both Gretton

1877
12 Dec: JINKS, John (RL) and Mary Ann BOON, both Gretton

1878
22 Jan: BLABER, John (RL) and Eliza SMITH, both Gretton

1879
17 Jul: PRENTICE, William (ED) and Anne WARNER, both Gretton

21 Jul: MANN, Noah (RL) and Frances WYMAN, both Gretton

I did not note the fathers or witnesses. All of these men had come from away to work on the railway. John Roodaway and his bride were both living in Gretton huts. John Shone was 54, and a widower, Mary Anne was not of a local family. Mary Ann Boon, Anne Warner and Francis Wyman were all Gretton girls, as was Eliza Smith née Boon, a 25-year-old widow. The first son of John and Mary Ann Jinks was buried on 1 December 1878, and the daughter of John and Elizabeth Blaber baptised on the same day.

Railway families appearing in Corby Baptism Register

Corby was at this time a small Northamptonshire village in Rockingham Forest. We have seen in earlier chapters that an estimated one thousand men worked on the deep cuttings and the tunnel between Corby and Gretton parishes, and here the men stayed for the longest time. The Corby Registers are particularly interesting, for they give the locations of some of the hut settlements in the parish. Rev P. B. Harris was the rector, and he has supplied other details that have proved most helpful – did he have an eye for posterity, one wonders?

BLAKE, John and Esther, Corby Wood   E
   s   John
CAMPBELL, Edward and Nellie, Corby   F
   s   Cecil
COLLIER Edmund and Matilda,
  Corby Wood   Ex
   s   Harry
CLEAVER, William and Elizabeth,
  Corby Wood   RL
   s   William

DICKENS, James Jabez and Jane,
  Corby Wood   TK
   s   Frederick Thomas
FARMER, Harry and Emma,
  Corby Wood   BM
   s   George Henry
   d   Emma Jane
FLATMAN, Samuel and Elizabeth,
  Corby   G
   d   Roseanne Amelia
FORBES, Peter and Helen Charlotte,
  Corby   En
   s   Archibald
   d   Agnes
   s   Sidney
GOTHIER(?), Thomas and Anne,
  Corby Wood   RL
   s   George William
   s   John Thomas
GRAY, Samuel and Elizabeth, Corby   RL
   s   Samuel
HARDING, William and Clara Georgiana,
  Corby Wood   M
   s   George Henry
KING, Samuel James and
  Mary Anne Bonney, Oakley Road   ED
   d   Florence
LATTIMORE, William and Emma,
  Corby Wood   RL
   d   Kate Emily
MARCH, Edward and Sarah Anne,
  Corby Wood   BM
   s   Oswald
   d   Ada Maud Bess
MEADE, William and Elizabeth   E
   d   Ellen Matilda
MERCER, Herbert and Elizabeth,
  Corby Wood   BM
   d   Sarah Elizabeth
METTON, James and Jane, Corby   BM
   d   Elizabeth Corby
PEARCE, John and Eliza   RL
   d   Charity Eliza Mary
PROWSE, Richard and Elizabeth,
  Corby Wood   Ex
   d   Fanny Corby
SCOTT, John Rutherford and Maggie   EF
   s   Thomas James Peter
SPURLOCK(?), John and Emily,
  Corby   ED
   s   Samuel

STANFORD, John and Harriett,
  Corby Wood   RL
    d   Eliza
    d   Elizabeth
STEVENS, John and Sarah Anne,
  Corby Wood   BM
    s   Walter
    s   Charles Alfred
    s   William
HEAD, Thomas and Sarah Ann,
  Pen Green   Ex
    s   Thomas
TOMLIN, Walter and Esther Maria,
  Corby   guard
    d   Emma Maria
TURNER, Henry and Emma,
  Corby Wood   RL
    s   Tom
WALLON(?), W. Henry and Eliza,
  Corby Wood   RL
    s   Thomas Henry
    d   Sarah Jane
    s   Thomas Henry
    s   John Thomas
WARSOM(?), James & Suzzanah,
  Corby   TK
    s   John Henry
WAYMAN, James and Eliza,
  Corby Wood   E
    s   Charles
    d   Ada
WEBSTER, Samuel and Martha, Corby   M
    s   Samuel John
WHALEY, James and Mary Anne, Corby RL
    d   Beatrice Annie
WHITE, Tom and Sarah Jane, Corby   RHK
    s   James
WILSON, William and Lydia   RL
    s   Herbert
WILSON, George and Harriett, Corby RL
    s   John William
WRIGHT, Alfred and Emma, Corby   RL
    s   Alfred

Mr Tomlin, the guard, had a note by his entry: 'Long Eaton now at Corby'. Mr Whaley, the railway labourer, also had a note: 'Nottingham and Bungay now at Corby'. Alfred and Emma Wright had 'Snatchell Lodge' by their entry, so they lived just north of Great and Little Oakley.

Corby burials of railway people from the Register

BRHC signifies Bank Railway Huts, Corby; CB Corby Brickyard; CW Corby Wood; ORH Oakley Road Huts; RHGB Railway Huts, Greeton Brook; and TL Thorny Lane.

22 Nov 1875	Thomas Franklin (14 months), RHGB
22 Nov 1875	Flora Wilmot (16 months), BRHC
23 Apr 1876	Railway man lodging at Glithero's (76)
30 Apr 1876	Clara Webster (10), ORH
3 Jun 1876	James Cogil(?) (25), RHGB
2 Jul 1876	Thomas White
8 Sep 1876	Jasper Rice (40)
13 Dec 1876	John McKenzie
? ? 1877	Eliza Anne Goddard (2 weeks), CW
5 Jul 1877	Thomas Hammond Elizabeth Baynham (32), ORH
14 Jul 1877	George Patrick (29)
23 Aug 1877	Stephen Griffiths (41)
24 Dec 1878	George Turner, TL
26 Jan 1879	Harriett Elizabeth Hibbs (32) Francis Thomas Payne (19 months), CB
6 Feb 1879	William Harris (25), CB

Greeton Brook Huts (not Gretton as I first thought) was a small settlement near the ventilation shaft closest to the south portal of the tunnel. Rev Thomas Addison, of Gretton, buried the unnamed railway man 'lodging at Glithero's'. Several of these deaths were the result of accidents, which was noted briefly in the Register: George Patrick was accidentally killed in the tunnel; Stephen Griffiths was accidentally killed in the railway cutting; and Thomas Hammond, George Turner and Jasper Rice were also all accidentally killed, but it was not recorded where or how. The circumstances of Thomas White's death are described in Chapter 10. By the entry for John McKenzie are the words: 'Found dead on Oakley Road in Corby Parish near new railway bridge.' There was another mysterious entry in 1876: 'A man, name unknown, commonly called Darkie or Black Frank, was found dead in the brickyard. Buried by Coroner's order.' William Harris was one of the very few railway workers out of the hundreds I have found who had 'navigator' as his occupation. As we saw earlier, Harriet Elizabeth Hibbs 'died it is supposed by her husband's hand'.

Corby marriages of railway people from the Register

1876
16 Apr: FOX, Thomas Cooke (19) (BL), Medbourne and Sarah Ann Bailey (24)

1879
20 Feb: TURNER, Charles (21) (RL), Thorny Lane, and Alice Kate Robinson (20)

For some reason I did not take note of the witnesses. Medbourne is in Leicestershire, and was on the route of the GNR line under construction, discussed earlier when the rivals for the territory were considered.

Railway families appearing in Great Oakley Baptism Register

DICKSON, William & Ellen   ED
    s   George Henry
HOSKINS, William and Anna   missionary
    d   Eliza
SEVENOAKS, William Frederick
    and Louisa Mary   RC
    d   Gertrude Anne
    d   Grace Matilda

Although there are only three families in this group, two raise questions for which at present I have no answer. I do not know whether Mr Hoskins the missionary was seconded to the railway or whether he had come home from abroad. Mr Dickson, although based at Great Oakley, had 'New England' in his entry. Mr Sevenoaks was one of the railway cashiers.

Great Oakley burials of railway people from the Register

30 Dec 1875   Susan Powell (38),
                Great Oakley Railway Huts

10 Feb 1876   William Brown (53),
                Great Oakley Railway Huts
28 Jun 1876   James Edwards (40),
                Great Oakley Railway Huts

It was disappointing not to find a reference to William Thomas Winfield, who, as already mentioned, had a fine memorial stone erected by his fellow workers in Great Oakley churchyard, as illustrated in Chapter 4. I have still not discovered how he died, or why he was held in such high regard.

There were no marriages of railway people in the Great Oakley Register.

Railway families appearing in Little Oakley Baptism Register

?, George and Louisa,
    Railway Huts Oakley   RL
    s   William John

There were no obvious railway burials or marriages registered.

The **Geddington** Registers were also looked at, but yielded no obvious railway people.

Railway families appearing in Rushton Baptism Register

DUMMETT(?),
    Matthew and Elizabeth Jane   RL
    s   Frederick John
PANTER, Samuel and Maria   PL
    d   Hannah Maria
    d   Rosina
SIMMONS, Tom and Mary   railway guard
    d   Edith Eva
STARKEY,
    William and Sarah Jane   pointsman
    s   John William
WOOLMER, George and Sarah Anne   PL
    d   Anne Elizabeth
    s   Frederick
WOOLMER, John and Celia   RL
    d   Sarah Elizabeth

Mr Simmons, the railway guard, had 'Litchurch, Derby' in his entry.

Such are the details of railway families gleaned from the Registers of the villages directly along the route of the railway works. From these lists it will be seen that the majority of those employed were railway labourers or miners. In spite of the widely held opinion that they were all Irish, and people still come up to me expressing it, I have found only two possible Irish names along the whole line. It could be argued that if any of the labour force did come from Ireland, they would probably be Roman Catholic and would thus not appear in the parish records. True, but surely if an Irish contingent was present some names would have appeared during the research into accidents, illness or crime, so I dismiss that myth as far as the Kettering to Manton line is concerned. Despite all these pages of names, but a small proportion of the workforce is represented. There were many hundreds who did not marry here, or have their children baptised, or were buried. We must remember also that men walked in to the works from other villages nearby – Wing and Preston, Morcott and Bisbrooke, Liddington and Rockingham, Newton and Glendon – and I have not included these. Most of all we must remember the truly anonymous ones, who came for a few days or weeks, then moved on. No one will ever know how many of them there were, for they left nothing but their work to show that they had been there at all.

13

EPILOGUE

In December 1879 the press announced that the new line of railway between Kettering and Manton was opened for goods traffic, and by the end of January both the Kettering to Manton and the Melton Mowbray to Nottingham stretches were carrying passengers. From now on we must consider these lines as one, for the Midland Railway Company's enterprise was now accomplished, except for the necessary extensions to the existing stations. Also up and running at this time, it must be said, was the Great Northern's new line from Newark to Market Harborough.

In January 1880 the press referred to the 'energy, public spirit, and reforming proclivities' that distinguished the Midland from all other companies. In an official pamphlet, extracts from which were published in the *Mercury* and the *Journal*, the Midland line was spoken of as:

'...one of the great trunk rails that has opened up in the heart of England to the requirements of commerce, and the use and convenience of the great travelling public. By immense and unwavering energy it has created a close union between the activities of the great metropolis, and all the most essential and representative centres of England. One of its feeders stands at Liverpool, the great watergate for America; another finds an opening through Carlisle, and gathers its traffic through the ever growing and energetic city of Glasgow; a third branches away to the east, and finds its terminus beneath the shadow of Edinburgh Castle; a fourth sweeps away

to the west, and embraces the commercial necessities of Bristol and the fashionable centre of Bath... Far and wide, through every description of scenery, and through every variety of English life, the great railway pushes its way.'

The Melton to Nottingham section eased the problem of the huge mineral and goods traffic at Leicester, and, linked together by the old Syston to Peterborough railway, the line between Manton and Kettering enabled the 'immense mineral treasures lying around Mansfield and along the Erewash Valley, to be conveyed with great dispatch and directness into the ever-growing maw of the metropolis...' And, as we have seen, the building of the Kettering to Manton line revealed its own treasure of iron ore, bringing to the district industry, employment and prosperity. In June the Midland Company commenced a service of through trains from Nottingham to London via Melton and Kettering, and soon the line regularly carried the Scottish express.

The press described both the advantages and the scenic beauty when the first fast trains from Nottingham, Manton and Kettering to London began to run:

'The line will undoubtedly become popular with business men travelling from London to the North, and ease the trains passing through Leicester and Loughborough without unfavourably affecting the service between those towns and the metropolis and the north. The line itself passes through one of the most lovely parts of the Midlands, if not of England. Traversing the valley of the Welland an extensive stretch of the richest pastoral scenery bursts upon the eye of the passenger, and the country between Melton and Nottingham is by no means uninteresting. Considerable difficulty was experienced in making the road, as may be gathered from the fact that 3,000 men were fully employed on it, and the cost has been heavy, in consequence of the length of tunnels which had to be made, the cuttings pierced, and the magnificent viaduct in the valley of the Welland, which is about a mile long...'

Many modern writers have charted the rise, progress and decline of the railway system during the 20th century. I do not consider it to be part of my brief to go into it, for it has been very well documented. The industry at Corby has also changed, and with it the mineral and commercial traffic. Suffice to say that the Kettering to Manton line is still in use, though stations have closed and passenger traffic is limited to high days and holidays, or when work takes place elsewhere on the line.

The builders

Almost up to the time of going to press, I had been unable to find any information about Lucas & Aird, other than Barrett's reference to 'the well-known contractors'. Very late in the day, I came up with 'John Arid & Sons' of London, and further to this found them in connection with the railway. I speculated that if 'Arid' was an ongoing printing error, I may have found Mr Aird, so continued on that basis. Then Mr Lucas came into the picture. I found that 'Lucas and Arid' exchanged a new contract with the Midland Railway Company to complete the Kettering to Manton line, then much delayed by the weather (we looked into how the weather had hindered the progress in Chapter 9). It would seem that a typing error has been perpetuated here. One way or the other, I am sure that Mr Arid and Mr Aird are one and the same.

Barlow, Son, & Baker was the civil engineering firm responsible for the survey, and Mr C. B. Baker and Mr Crawford Barlow carried it out. Their work not only determined the actual route but also assessed the

The Peterborough line platforms...

The line opens: Manton station in Midland Railway days, looking from the tunnel. Curving round to the left, the original Syston to Peterborough line heads east, with the new line to Kettering branching to the right. *Pam Voss, Gretton Local History Society*

...and the Kettering line platforms at Manton, photographed in 1963. *H. C. Casserley*

Above left and above Midland days at Gretton: Walter Adams, signalman, moved from Wellingborough to Gretton in 1901, and his son Stanley (*above*) worked as a porter at Manton station in the 1920s. *Alma Woolley, Gretton Local History Society*

Left Indian summer: Station Master Pomphret and porter Elsie Smith tend the award-winning garden at Gretton in 1961. *Clifford Kerfoot, Gretton Local History Society*

Top right The track diagram from Gretton signal box, showing the layout from 1957 to 1966. *Arthur and Elisabeth Jordan*

Above right Harringworth and Geddington stations closed as early as 1948, then Gretton and Corby followed suit in April 1966 when the line lost its passenger service; subsequent attempts to re-open Corby station have proved unsuccessful. Manton lingered until June 1966. Here is the last train at Gretton. *Clifford Kerfoot, Gretton Local History Society*

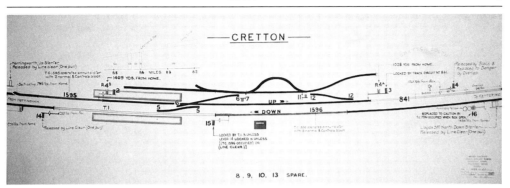

Right The south end of the line, at Glendon South Junction, north of Kettering, in 1994, with track rationalisation in progress. The Midland Railway's main line to Leicester and the North is on the left, with the Manton line curving away from the goods lines on the right; previously the goods lines had continued north round the corner as far as Glendon North Junction. *Author*

Above Happily the line is still open for freight traffic, and occasional special and diversionary passenger trains. *Author*

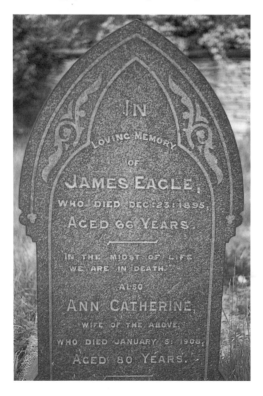

earthworks required to maintain the gradients to a minimum, and from this assessment the tenders were put out. Benjamin (later Sir Benjamin) Baker was a most distinguished engineer. After the Tay Bridge disaster in 1879, he designed the Forth Bridge, and among other railway works, was, with his partner John Fowler, engineer for the first London tube railway. He was also engaged on the dams on the River Nile. Mr Crawford Barlow was the resident civil engineer for the Kettering to Manton project.

Mr James Eagle was appointed by Lucas & Aird as their local agent, responsible for the whole works, until in 1877 he went to Egypt to take up a large contract there. This was probably the Nile dams project, because of the connections already touched upon. Meanwhile his daughter had married into a Gretton family. By 1881 Mr Eagle must have returned to England, for according to the

Left In the churchyard extension at Gretton is the grave of Mr James Eagle, local agent for the contractors until the spring of 1877, and who returned to spend his retirement in Gretton. *Author*

Census he was living with his wife at Clitheroe, Lancashire. On his retirement they returned to Gretton, where he became a parish councillor and was largely responsible for introducing oil street lighting in the village, which, as already mentioned, was lit for the first time on Christmas Eve 1895, though sadly Mr Eagle had died the day before, aged 66. His wife, Ann Catherine, died 13 years later, aged 80. Mr Eagle and his wife are both buried at Gretton and a handsome headstone marks their grave. Their descendants live in the district still.

The Bishop and the Missionaries

The Right Reverend William Connor Magee (1821-91) was Lord Bishop of Peterborough for 22 years, and was one of the greatest orators of his day, as famous for his sermons from the pulpit as his speeches in the House of Lords. Many of his sermons, speeches and lectures were published. In 1868, as Dean of the Chapel Royal, Dublin, and at the same time Dean of Cork, he preached the opening sermon in St Patrick's Cathedral, Dublin, when the Church Congress was held there.

His theme was 'The Breaking Net', and contained these words:

'Spread, as she is, all over the nation, bound to supply all its spiritual needs as they arise, the Church is exposed to sudden strains on her resources by all the rapid changes in the distribution or even in the habits of the people... The growth of some new hive of human industry makes from time to time fresh and sudden demands upon her strength. Suddenly the net of some quiet country parish is filled with the influx of a great multitude; the village becomes a town ... almost in a day; and then the net is strained to breaking...'

A few months later, the Prime Minister, Mr Disraeli, recommended his promotion to the see of Peterborough, and he was consecrated as Bishop on 15 November 1868. He made a series of brilliant speeches in the House of Lords, and his reputation as a powerful orator matched his fame as a preacher of great wisdom and humanity. He was concerned about the plight of the people drawn to the growing towns, and instituted among other things new churches in Northampton and Leicester. The reconstruction of the tower of Peterborough Cathedral also took place in his time.

In January 1891 he was chosen to succeed Dr William Thomson as Archbishop of York, and was enthroned in York Minster on 17 March. Only a few weeks later he went to London to attend a committee of the House of Lords, fell victim to the influenza epidemic, and died. His funeral took place on 5 May 1891, seven weeks after his enthronement. His grave is in the burial-ground of Peterborough Cathedral, and inside is a fine monument and photograph. His wife, three sons and three daughters survived him. The two oldest children died young. It was said that the Bishop was a household name in England, and was the man the navvies claimed as their own – the 'Navvies' Bishop'.

Before the call to the Bishop of Peterborough's Railway Mission, the Reverend Daniel William Barrett (1851-1928) had been curate of Bierley, West Yorkshire (1872-73) and Waltham-on-the-Wolds, Leicestershire (1873-76). In December 1878, as the Railway Mission was drawing to its natural end, he was licensed to the parish of Lyddington, Rutland, a living that had fallen on hard times due to the neglect of the previous incumbent. Although he was there but a short time, under his care the church prospered. He showed the same enthusiasm at Lyddington as he had on the Mission, as illustrated in this report published both in the *Stamford Mercury* and the *Grantham Journal* in April 1879:

'Lyddington: During the last few weeks there have been some great improvements in the church of Lyddington, near Uppingham. By the energy of the Vicar, the Rev D. W. Barrett, Curate in Charge, and by the kind assistance of many liberal friends, two stoves have been placed in the church, which very effectually heat it, and it is now well lighted with numerous lamps suspended from the roof. The organ is now in the chancel. The gallery, in which it formerly stood, has been taken down, which allows the fine arch in the west end of the nave to be seen to much better advantage. The pulpit, which was a very ugly one, has been greatly improved.'

About that time he had become Secretary to the Navvy Mission Society, following the death of Rev Lewis Moule Evans. An account of a drawing-room meeting (probably the inaugural meeting) that took place on 16 May 1879 appears as Appendix D in Barrett's *Life and Work Among the Navvies*. A few weeks later, in June 1879, he preached his last sermon as Curate in Charge at Lyddington, having been appointed by the Bishop to the living of

Rev Daniel William Barrett in later life when he was Rector of All Saints, Holdenby, Northamptonshire. *Courtesy of Holdenby House*

Nassington-cum-Yarwell, Northamptonshire. That same month the new line from Seaton to Wansford was opened for goods traffic, and it will be remembered that navvies working on this line were at Seaton while Barrett was there. Of the three stations on the line after leaving Seaton, the last was at Nassington. Barrett baptised the children of four railway labourers on 7 September 1879, and in 1880 his own son, John Rendell Hattersley, was baptised by Rev A. M. Rendell, Rector of Coston, Leicestershire, who, it may be remembered, was the brother of Mrs Barrett. That same year *Life and Work Among the Navvies* was published to great acclaim, and eventually ran to four editions. There was to be another son and two daughters; in his obituary his family were named as Mr R. H. Barrett, Mr A. M. Barrett, Miss C. M. Barrett and Miss M. A. Barrett. He was at Nassington until 1887, and during that time was Rural Dean of Oundle. From 1887 to 1910 he was Rector of Chipping Barnet, and was also Chaplain of Chipping Barnet Union from 1889-1909, Rural Dean of Barnet 1893-1909, and Honorary Canon of St Albans 1905-10. His work *Sketches of Church Life* was published in 1902. In 1910 he became Rector of All Saints, Holdenby, Northamptonshire, and there he was until his death in 1928, his wife having died two years earlier. What follows is part of an article from the *Northampton Independent* of 19 September 1928:

'The late Canon Barrett: The death of the Rev Canon D. W. Barrett MA, the beloved Rector of Holdenby, has caused a profound shock and deep sorrow among all who knew him. It was only a few weeks ago that he announced his resignation and we all hoped that in his impending retirement at Woburn Sands he would be sufficiently restored to resume in his leisure the literary labours for which like his famous predecessor, the late Canon Cox, he was so well endowed. He would seem, however, to have had a premonition of his coming fate, for only a fortnight ago he wrote me a letter, which commenced, "I am getting too old and feeling too ill to continue my various publications." He was the author of several successful works, including *The Royal Prisoner of Holdenby*, for which there was a great demand. He took immense pains and trouble over that publication and made it a valuable addition to our local history. He discovered however, like all other historians, that all his researches and learned writing meant also a pecuniary sacrifice…

The late Canon Barrett had been Rector of Holdenby since 1910. He had previously held livings in Yorkshire, Leicestershire and at Nassington. At the request of the Bishop of Peterborough he took up a prolonged mission among railway navvies, and his experiences among them is embodied in his pamphlet *Life and Work Among the Navvies*, which has run into its fourth edition. To one of his culture and refinement, such work involved a stupendous sacrifice, for he had to overcome much ignorant and insulting opposition. The navvies, however, learnt to love and respect him, and he radiated life-long good influences. The reverend gentleman was an Honorary Canon of St Albans, and he leaves two daughters, who lived with him, and two sons.'

The daughter of a vicar, Mrs Elizabeth Garnett (1839-1920) was drawn towards missionary work as a child. She had been much moved by a sermon delivered at the dedication of a memorial to 23 men who died while working on a railway tunnel in Yorkshire. After the tragic death of her husband Charles, who, it is said, died on their honeymoon; she became deeply concerned with the lot of the navvies and their families. In 1875 she founded the Christian Excavators' Union, a mission that, like that of the Bishop of Peterborough, aimed to bring spiritual and practical help to the navvies and their families. Like Barrett, she worked with contractors to provide huts for spiritual needs, recreation, education and comfort.

Aware of how scattered and transient was the navvy population throughout the country, she brought out her 'Quarterly Letter to the

Mrs Garnett, navvy missionary and author, whose book gave me much insight into navvy life.

Navvies' in 1878. It carried lists of work in progress, news of deaths and missing persons and similar information, as well as mission matters and the Christian message. She was editor for 30 years. Typical of her class and times, Mrs Garnett was very active in the temperance movement. Her book *Our Navvies: a Dozen Years Ago and Today*, published in 1885, is a very revealing insight into all aspects of navvy life.

A memorial tablet in Ripon Cathedral reads:

'To the glory of God and in grateful memory of the devoted life and service of Elizabeth Garnett. She spent the greater portion of her days on earth in ministering to the spiritual and temporal needs of the navvy communities employed on public works in this country and abroad. In 1877 she was instrumental in founding in this city the Christian Excavators' Union and was widely beloved as the friend and a true sister in Christ. She led many to know and love the Master through her example of unwearied service.'

The navvies disperse

The works were at their height from June 1877 to June 1878, then, as Barrett wrote, there was a constant cessation of work taking place. The huge gangs of 70 or 80 grew less and less. Equipment, plant, spare huts and so on were sent away daily to other works. You might walk a mile along the tunnel top and hardly meet a soul, he said. The navvies became scattered again, far and wide, north and south, east and west. These were the days of the Empire and the Raj, so some went to India, to the Colonies, to New Zealand and Canada. Some stayed in the British Isles. A few years later I have no doubt that many of the Kettering to Manton navvies came back to the region to build the Great Central Railway.

And that is another story...

Lengthening shadows from the setting sun highlight the 82 arches of the Welland Viaduct, with the village of Harringworth beyond and the meandering River Welland in the foreground. *Arthur and Elisabeth Jordan collection*